VENICE AND AMSTERDAM

VENICE AND AMSTERDAM

A Study of Seventeenth-Century Elites

PETER BURKE

SECOND EDITION

Polity Press

The right of Peter Burke to be identified as author of this work has been
asserted in accordance with the Copyright, Designs and Patents Act 1988.

First published in 1994 by Polity Press in association with Blackwell Publishers.

Editorial office:
Polity Press
65 Bridge Street
Cambridge CB2 1UR, UK

Marketing and production:
Blackwell Publishers
108 Cowley Road
Oxford OX4 1JF, UK

238 Main Street
Cambridge, MA 02142, USA

ISBN 0 7456 1343 8
ISBN 0 7456 1324 1 (pbk)

A CIP catalogue record for this book is available from the British Library and
from the Library of Congress.

Typeset in 11 on 13 pt Sabon by Best-set Typesetter Ltd., Hong Kong
Printed in Great Britain by Hartnolls Ltd, Bodmin, Cornwall

This book is printed on acid-free paper.

A merchant is accustomed to employ his money chiefly in profitable projects; whereas a mere country gentleman is accustomed to employ it chiefly in expense. The one often sees his money go from him and return to him again with a profit: the other, when he parts with it, very seldom expects to see any more of it. Those different habits naturally affect their temper and disposition in every sort of business. A merchant is commonly bold; a country gentleman, a timid undertaker . . . The habits, beside, of order, economy and attention, to which mercantile business naturally forms a merchant, render him much fitter to execute, with profit and success, any project of improvement.

Adam Smith, Wealth of Nations, *bk III, ch. 4*

Contents

Illustrations

Between pp. 102 and 103

Acknowledgements

When working on the first edition, I incurred many debts. The necessary research in Venice and Amsterdam was made possible by the Leverhulme Trust which made me a Faculty Fellow in European Studies in 1972. The staff of the Archivio di Stato at Venice and the Gemeente Archief at Amsterdam, in particular Francesca Maria Tiepolo and the late Simon Hart, offered advice, information and encouragement. I also learned a good deal from discussions with Gaetano Cozzi, of Venice (whose publications are cited so frequently in this book); Brian Pullan, of Manchester; Koenrad Swart, of London; Ivo Schöffer, of Leiden; the late Charles Wilson, of Cambridge, and my friend Riccardo Steiner. Teaching a course at the University of Sussex on 'aristocracies and elites' led me to the subject in the first place, and discussions with the students taking it did a great deal to clarify my ideas. So did conversations with fellow-workers in Venice – Bill Brown, Alex Cowan, Oliver Logan, Ed Muir and Jim Williamson. Parts of this book were tried out on audiences at the Universities of Edinburgh and London, and at the Royal Historical Society's conference on 'Urban Civilization' at Oxford in 1972. A number of the suggestions made on these occasions proved most helpful. John Hale, Rupert Wilkinson and Maurice Temple Smith read the typescript and offered valuable suggestions for improvement.

In preparing the second edition of this book my greatest debt is to Herman Roodenburg, who compiled for me a bibliography of studies of Amsterdam published since 1974. I should also like to thank Ms Marijke Meier Drees for sending me a copy of her dissertation, Rudolf Dekker, S. A. C. Dudok van Heel, Florike Egmond and Leonard Forster for keeping me in touch with recent work on Dutch social and cultural history, and H. Quarles van Ufford for information about the Amsterdam elite's country estates. The lectures and seminars organized in Amsterdam on the occasion of the exhibition 'Amsterdam: Venice of the North' in 1991 revived my interest in the subject. I should also like to thank the organizers of these events for presenting me with a copy of Henri Havard's *Amsterdam et Venise*.

Introduction to the Second Edition

Twenty years have passed since I began work on seventeenth-century Venice and Amsterdam. In this time a considerable number of books and articles have been published on these two cities and their environments. Still more important, the way in which history is written has changed in significant ways. The purpose of this introductory essay is to offer a few personal comments on these changes (as well as on reactions to the first edition of this book), dealing in turn with three themes: the comparative approach, the study of elites and what is sometimes called 'the new cultural history'.

The comparative approach Comparative history was of course no new idea in the 1970s. It had been advocated and practised earlier in the century by historians of the calibre of the Belgian Henri Pirenne, the Frenchman Marc Bloch and the German Otto Hintze, while a journal devoted to the subject – *Comparative Studies in Society and History* – was founded in 1958 and continues to this day. I still believe in the value of this approach to history, and for essentially the same reasons.

In the first place, for a historian concerned with a particular society, the Netherlands for example, comparisons – and contrasts – with other parts of the world will allow him or her to notice certain features of that society which might otherwise have been missed, and equally important, to notice significant absences. In the second place, comparison is of great assistance in the search for explanation. One reason for writing this book, at a time when I was teaching sociology as well as history, was to try to test the conclusions of social theorists concerned with elites, from Vilfredo Pareto to C. Wright Mills.[1] In the words of the author of a distinguished recent study of the French, Russian and Chinese revolutions, comparative historical analysis makes possible a more rigorous approach, indeed 'serves as an ideal strategy for mediating between theory and history'.[2]

I have to admit that I expected comparative history to attract more interest and to develop more quickly than it in fact did in the 1970s and 1980s. In its original form this book was my own contribution to a series I edited for the publisher Maurice Temple Smith, which included one study of feudalism in northern France and in Japan, another on Byzantium and Bulgaria and a third on Britain and the USA since the Second World War.[3] The series came to an end largely because of the difficulty of finding potential authors, and the same problem arose when I tried to launch a similar series for Oxford University Press.

These experiences can be matched elsewhere. Even the articles published in *Comparative Studies in Society and History* generally focus on one region, and are comparative only by implication. Yet there are signs of change. On one side, an increasing number of sociologists are turning (or, more exactly, turning back) to history without abandoning the interest in comparative analysis so well exemplified by their masters Émile Durkheim and Max Weber. On the other, some historians are turning to comparison. Books as diverse in subject-matter and style as John Elliott's study of the rival statesmen Cardinal Richelieu and the Count-Duke of Olivares and Carlo Ginzburg's investigations into the myth of the witches' sabbath share a concern with the comparative method, while a project is afoot to write the history of the Netherlands from a comparative perspective.[4]

[1] For further reflections on the relation between history and sociological theory, see Burke (1992).
[2] Skocpol (1979).
[3] Lewis (1974); Browning (1975); Snowman (1977).
[4] Elliott (1984); Ginzburg (1989); Davids et al. (1988).

The trend to comparison is particularly visible among historians of Africa and Asia, perhaps because they are more deeply involved in the teaching of world history than specialists on Europe tend to be. A new series, Cambridge Studies in Comparative World History, both illustrates and encourages this trend. There is now a paper on comparative history in the Honour School of Modern History at Oxford. The subject appears to be moving at last from the margins to the mainstream.

Let us hope, then, that a historian or a group of historians will now undertake a more serious comparative study of Europe and its regions, a history of the cultural divisions into east and west, north and south, divisions which range from material life (oil versus butter, wine versus beer, and so on) to family structure, religion and political culture.[5] Such a study would enable us to decide whether the Cambridge anthropologist Alan Macfarlane's famous contrast between England and the Continent should be redefined as a contrast between north-west Europe and the south and east.[6] It is in this broader context that comparisons and contrasts between Venice and Amsterdam need to be located.

The study of elites   The study of elites in general, and urban patriciates in particular, has been attracting historians in increasing numbers in the last two decades, notably in Italy, Germany and the Netherlands (where, thanks to the late Daniel J. Roorda, it was incorporated in the collective research programme of the University of Leiden).[7] Relatively few historians have studied the culture and the mentalities as well as the wealth and power of these patriciates, with the exception of James Amelang's book on Barcelona in the sixteenth and seventeenth centuries.[8] The majority of these studies of elites employ quantitative methods, as one might have expected in an age of personal computers, and they base many of their conclusions on 'prosopography', or the collec-

---

[5]   A conference on 'The evolution of the relations between European regions (14th to 18th centuries)' was organized in Paris in 1992 by Antoni Mączak and Maarten Prak.

[6]   Macfarlane (1978).

[7]   Among many possible examples, see the collective volumes *Patriziati* (1978); Ehbrecht (1980); Tagliaferri (1984); Schilling and Diederiks (1985).

[8]   Amelang (1986).

tive biography of a social group. Among the advantages of this quantitative approach is that it facilitates comparisons between one elite and another.

Defining the group which is to be studied by these methods, however, remains problematic, as noted in the first edition of this book (below, p. 11). In the first place, the groups with most power, wealth and status generally overlap but rarely coincide.[9] As an illustration of this lack of fit between the three criteria for elite status one might take the obvious fact that the 563 individuals studied in this book are all men. The reason for the choice is of course that they held high office in societies in which high office was a male monopoly. On the other hand, their wives, daughters and sisters had some share in their status and to a lesser extent in their wealth, so that it could reasonably be argued that they should have made rather more frequent appearances in this essay.

Problems also arise in the case of power, which is a considerably more elusive object of study than wealth or even status. Contrasts between official position and unofficial influence are only to be expected. In Venice and Amsterdam alike it is difficult to find what have been called 'the frontiers of the patriciate'. In Venice, for instance, the new recruits of the later seventeenth century were certainly wealthy, but it took considerable time for them to acquire status and even longer for them to exercise power.

Conversely, the hundred leading political figures of Venice listed by a contemporary in 1675 included some who were not particularly wealthy.[10] A similar point might be made in the Dutch case. A recent study of the regents of Leiden in the eighteenth century revealed that they did not monopolize status symbols such as land, country houses and coaches in the same way as they monopolized power. Only half the regents owned country houses, and half the country houses in the region were owned by other inhabitants of Leiden.[11] In Amsterdam it would be even more unwise to assume that large fortunes were a monopoly of the members of the Town Council. One has only to think of a few of the Sephardi Jews of Amsterdam, Antonio Lopes Suasso for

---

[9] Cf. Burke (1993b).
[10] Cowan (1982, 1986).
[11] Prak et al. (1985).

example, whose wealth can be gauged from the fact that they were engaged in supplying armies with food, pay and munitions. This elite of outsiders with international connections deserves a prosopographical study in its own right.[12]

To complicate matters still further, the social frontiers we are looking for were shifting during the period itself. The regents of Amsterdam were much more of an elite, in the sense of an exclusive social group, at the end of the period than they were at the beginning. It is unlikely that they saw themselves as different from their business colleagues in 1580, but extremely probable that they did so in the later seventeenth century, when an English visitor, William Carr (presumably reproducing the conventional wisdom of the Dutch at this time), remarked, 'The old severe and frugal way of living is now almost quite out of date in Holland . . . The Hollanders now build stately palaces, have their delightful gardens and houses of pleasure.'[13] This is surely an important part of what is meant by the term 'aristocratization', coined in this context by Pieter Geyl but launched by Daniel J. Roorda, and sometimes criticized as if it meant that the regent class had literally turned into a nobility, rather than simply imitating aspects of the noble style of life.[14]

In Venice too the movement from trade to land, discussed in the final chapter of this book, led to a division within the patriciate. The rich or senatorial families – an elite within the elite – were coming to distinguish themselves more and more sharply from the rest.[15] It was against this tendency towards a 'republic of princes' that the noble 'demagogue' Renier Zen* protested so forcefully in the 1620s in the name of republican equality (equality, that is, within the patriciate).

There was a similar tendency in sixteenth-century Florence and also in Venice's sister-republic of Genoa.[16] Genoa has recently been the object of a number of important studies which concentrate on the history of its ruling class in the sixteenth and seventeenth centuries.[17] Here too it was claimed that a few patrician

---

[12]   There is a brief account in Israel (1985), 127ff.
[13]   Carr (1688), 102.
[14]   Roorda (1964); Dijk and Roorda (1971).
[15]   Scazzoso (1985); Cozzi (1986).
[16]   Kellenbenz (1958).
[17]   Grendi (1976); Costantini (1978); Savelli (1981); Bitossi (1976, 1990).

families, such as the branches of the Pallavicino and Spinola clans who lent money to the King of Spain, behaved as if they were superior to the rest. In Genoa in the early seventeenth century the spokesman for the traditional republican values of liberty, equality and frugality was a certain Andrea Spinola, a minor patrician nicknamed by his contemporaries 'the Philosopher'. His reflections on his own time have survived in a number of manuscript copies, suggesting that they circulated privately in his own day. It is not surprising to discover that Spinola admired not only ancient Rome and Sparta but the modern Swiss and Dutch republics as well.

The new cultural history   Quantitative history was probably at its height in the 1950s and 1960s. In the 1970s and 1980s there was something of a reaction against it, together with a rejection of economic determinism. Marxist and non-Marxist historians alike discovered the relative autonomy of culture, a term which came to be employed more and more frequently in a wide, anthropological sense rather than restricted to the world of literature and the arts. There has also been a rise of interest in historical anthropology (to some extent at the expense of sociology) and in 'microhistory', in other words the intensive study of communities and groups too small to make quantitative methods useful. The aim of the microhistorians is more to recover the experience of social change than to analyse its 'causes', and the basic assumption is that of the autonomy – within limits of course – of ordinary people, who are increasingly seen as subjects and not as mere objects of history.[18] The interest in new topics has been associated with the exploitation of new sources, among them images, which are not only used to decorate or illustrate the text but form part of the argument.

Written in the early 1970s, this study was already affected by the movements just described. It is a kind of microhistory in the sense of being concerned with a small enough group, 563 individuals, for it to be possible to study them one by one (their names will be marked by asterisks whenever they appear). Since the group is small, it becomes a little less dangerous than usual to

---

[18] Le Roy Ladurie (1975) and Ginzburg (1976), models since followed by scores (if not hundreds) of studies. General discussion by G. Levi (1991).

attempt 'total history' in Fernand Braudel's sense of the term, studying and linking different aspects of social life in a similar way to social anthropologists, who also work on a small scale. Indeed, the essay borrows concepts from social anthropology on occasion, most obviously Max Gluckman's idea of 'the peace in the feud' (below, p. 38) and Erving Goffman's concepts of 'front' and 'the presentation of self' (pp. 111ff). It is concerned with culture in the wide sense, sometimes from the angle of historical psychology, as in the case of the discussion of the consequences of early weaning (pp. 85, 89), which juxtaposes seventeenth-century sources to the hypotheses of Melanie Klein and Erik Erikson. Published in 1974, the book appeared too soon to make use of the French anthropologist and sociologist Pierre Bourdieu's idea of 'habitus', in other words a cultural style which includes posture and gesture as well as mentality, but its discussion of the noble style of life pointed in the same direction.[19]

The book makes obvious use of quantitative methods, but it also draws on literary sources such as the poems of Cristoforo Ivanovitch and Jan Vos, the operas of Francesco Cavalli, the plays of Joost van den Vondel and images ranging from engravings and drawings of nobles shooting fowl on the Venetian lagoons to the paintings of the Amsterdam civic militia by Rembrandt and Bartholomeus van de Helst. Arguments sometimes depend on this visual evidence, from the pellets used by Venetian patricians to stun the fowl they hunted to the shift of Amsterdam regents to a more hedonistic value-system, symbolized by the change from black to coloured clothes, illustrated by a painting by Cornelis Troost (see cover). Given the clues offered by pictorial detail, a historian can only regret that Pietro Malombra's painting of the Venetian political market-place, or *broglio*, has been lost.[20]

The use of images as sources for social history is indispensable (how else, for example, can one reconstruct seventeenth-century posture or gesture?), but it is no easy matter. Today I am less sure than I once was that the existence of portraits of small children (including some members of the de Graeff family who died in infancy and were painted in their swaddling clothes, plate 9) is a

---

[19]   Bourdieu (1972), 78–87. On Italian gesture, cf. Burke (1991a).
[20]   Ridolfi (1648), vol. 2, 157.

sign that they were taken seriously as individuals, rather than displayed as a part of the family. Before we can read an image with any confidence, we need to know why it was produced. For instance, in the case of the portrait of Willem van Loon,* later burgomaster, painted when the sitter was two years old, it may well be significant that the child is wearing mourning dress.[21] In the case of some paintings of the civic militia in which the figures pay more attention to their knives, forks and glasses than to their weapons, we need to remember that they represent not everyday life but a particular event, the celebration of the peace of Westphalia in 1648, which put an end to what the Dutch call the Eighty Years' War.

All the same, historians cannot afford to neglect the evidence of visual sources. They need to avoid or overcome the false dichotomy between quantitative and qualitative methods, like those between sociology and anthropology, the micro-level and the macro-level, understanding from within and analysis from outside. It is necessary, in short, to go beyond the apparently opposing positions and to achieve a synthesis. I tried to do this in 1974 and I am still trying to do so today.

Of course I would write this book somewhat differently if I were beginning it now. With one exception, however, the difference would take the form of developing in more detail approaches which were sketched in 1974, rather than of introducing something new. That exception is popular culture, the subject to which I turned after completing *Venice and Amsterdam* in 1973, and which I would define as the attitudes, values and mentalities of ordinary people, expressed, embodied, and symbolized in texts, artefacts and performances.[22]

It may sound a little strange to suggest that a study of elites should discuss popular culture, so it may be useful to try to explain why. Whether or not there are periods when the culture of the elite is completely distinct from that of ordinary people, the seventeenth century was not one of them. The elites of Europe at this period might reasonably be described as 'bi-cultural'. They had access to a culture which ordinary people could not share, a

[21] A detail pointed out to me by Herman Roodenburg.
[22] Burke (1978).

culture which included classical literature, baroque art and what was known as the 'mechanical philosophy' (or, as we call it, 'science'). On the other hand, they participated in popular culture as a second culture. They knew and often appreciated popular artefacts and performances. If they had not done so, they would have found it difficult to communicate with their wives and daughters, who were generally excluded from much of the 'high' culture of the time.

In any case, we know of Venetian patricians who participated in Carnival, just as we know that the poet Pieter C. Hooft (son of Cornelis P. Hooft*) enjoyed folksongs. Jacob Cats was a member of the ruling class of Zeeland, a successful lawyer who rose to the position of grand pensionary of Holland, but his poems very quickly became part of Dutch popular culture.[23] In the Dutch Republic the barriers between learned culture and popular culture seem to have been particularly easy to penetrate, so much so that it may be useful to speak of a 'middle-class culture' between the two, provided that we do not imagine it as a culture exclusive to merchants or as marked off in a clear and distinct manner from 'high' and 'low' cultures.[24] The example of Aernout van Overbeke is instructive in this respect. A member of the ruling class who lived in Leiden and The Hague, his collection of 2,440 anecdotes or jests suggests that he was culturally amphibious, moving without difficulty between the high and the low.[25]

The history of popular culture merges into the history of the everyday, *Alltagsgeschichte* as it is called in Germany, an approach which is close to historical anthropology. The everyday already had its place in the first edition of this book, but the pages devoted to it could easily have been extended. Among the topics which I now regret having treated so briefly (and on which I have since undertaken research) are conspicuous consumption, manners, language, gesture and sociability.[26]

In the case of consumption, it would be particularly easy to extend the section on art patronage and also on collecting, a

[23] Huizinga (1932), 65–7; Renier (1944), 145–61;
[24] Burke (1978), ch. 2; Burke (1979); Deursen (1978–80).
[25] Overbeke (1991).
[26] Burke (1982, 1987, 1991a).

subject on which much has been written in the last twenty years and to which a specialist periodical is now devoted, *The Journal of the History of Collections*.[27] In the case of Venice, it might, for example, be of interest to point out that Marcantonio Barbaro* was not only an important patron on his own behalf but an artistic adviser to the government who was concerned with the funeral monument to the late Doge Nicolò da Ponte,* for instance, and the design of the Rialto bridge.[28] One might add that Carlo Ridolfi, whose account of Venetian art is a major source for the patronage of the elite, was encouraged to write his book by Doge Francesco Erizzo,* or that the artistic enthusiasms of Nicolò Sagredo* extended to Salvator Rosa and Carlo Maratta as well as to Poussin.[29]

In the case of Amsterdam patronage, it might be worth pointing out that the classical scholar J. C. Graevius dedicated a work to Joannes Hudde* and Joan Corver;* that the playwright Thomas Asselijn dedicated his play *Den Grooten Kurieen* (1657), which deals with two 'burgomasters' of ancient Rome, to Cornelis de Vlaming van Outshoorn,* burgomaster of Amsterdam, and his *Mas Anjello* (1668), on the subject of urban revolt, to the son of another burgomaster, Cornelis van Vlooswijck.* Again, burgomaster Gerrit Reynst* owned not only a magnificent house but also a fine collection of pictures, some of them Italian, singled out in a contemporary description of Amsterdam as 'famous throughout the city'.[30] The town houses built for members of the elite by the architect Adriaan Dorsman also deserve to be mentioned.

More important than adding still more concrete examples, however, is refining their interpretation. For instance, the increasing concern with the arts on the part of the regents of Amsterdam should probably be viewed as a sign of their aristocratization, while the taste of some of them for artists from Italy, France or the southern Netherlands (such as Artus Quellin) reveals their withdrawal from participation in the popular culture of their day.[31]

I would now place more emphasis (following the theories of Norbert Elias) on what the patricians (or at least a group within

27   Impey and Macgregor (1985); Pomian (1987).
28   Gaeta (1964).
29   Rosa (1939), no. 22; Bellori (1672), 586f.
30   On Asselijn, Meier Drees (1989), esp. 20ff, 147; Zesen (1664), 361.
31   Cf. Price (1974), ch. 6.

the patriciate) perceived at the time as 'the duty to live magnificently' (*l'obbligazione di viver con fasto*), as a seventeenth-century
Neapolitan lawyer once put it, in order to uphold the honour of
their families. In a similar manner (following the theories of Pierre
Bourdieu), I would place more stress on conspicuous consumption
as a strategy for distinguishing a family from its social equals (and
rivals) as well as from its social inferiors.[32] Old and new rich alike
engaged in this kind of competition. One might think that when
the newly ennobled Vincenzo Fini* had his name placed on the
façade of the Venetian Church of San Moisè, in the 1660s, he was
acting like a vulgar *nouveau riche*, but it should be added that he
was doing no more than follow the example of such papal families
as the Farnese, Borghese and Aldobrandini in Rome, Frascati and
elsewhere.

The long-standing tension between the traditional republican
and mercantile ideal of frugality and the noble virtue of magnificence also needs to be emphasized, as well as the gradual shift in
the course of the seventeenth century from one ideal to the other.
The comparative study of Italian cities suggests that the Venetian
patricians were relatively slow to shift in this direction, confirming
the hypothesis that what most encouraged this style of consumption was the example of the prince and his court.[33]

Courts were also influential in the spread of new standards of
behaviour, manners or etiquette (*civilité* was a term commonly
used at the time, even outside France). Here too it was Norbert
Elias who drew attention to the importance of the long-term rise
of 'civilization' (in the sense of self-control), as well as to the
spread of such material forms of civilization as the handkerchief
and the fork.[34] More recently, under the inspiration of Michel
Foucault, a number of historians have turned to the social history
of the body and the 'discipline' imposed on it, not only in armies
and prisons but also in schools for elites. The history of gesture is
increasingly recognized as part of sociocultural history. So is the
history of the dance, which taught the young nobles self-control
and helped inculcate a style of deportment (or, as Bourdieu would

---

[32]   N. Elias (1969); Bourdieu (1979).
[33]   Burke (1982).
[34]   N. Elias (1939), vol. 1.

say, a corporal 'habitus'), which enabled them to distinguish themselves from their social inferiors.[35]

Social historians have learned from the sociolinguists, or the
ethnographers of communication, to pay attention to the meaning
of the decision to speak in one variety of language rather than
another. Clothes too are being taken more seriously by historians
than they used to be, and studied – like other aspects of material
culture – as a form of communication. Even humour is now
recognized to have a history, to form part of the history of mentalities.[36]

Thanks to these new approaches to sociocultural history, I
would now write about the style of life of the elites of Venice and
Amsterdam in a somewhat different manner. Rereading the first
edition, I was a little surprised to discover that I had actually made
brief references to many of these topics: to the silence and the slow
gait of the Venetian patricians, for instance (pp. 72, 73), to the
changing forms of wit (pp. 122, 124) and to the symbolism of
the shift from black to coloured clothes (p. 78) as well as to the
notorious cleanliness of the Dutch (pp. 89–90).

All the same, these brief references could easily be expanded,
and some recent studies point in this direction. Pieter Spierenburg,
for example, has noted the growing number of editions of treatises
on manners in the Dutch Republic in the seventeenth century,
notably Antoine de Courtin's *Nouveau traité de civilité*. Simon
Schama has suggested that the Dutch concern with cleanliness,
especially the scrubbing and polishing of houses and furniture, had
a symbolic meaning, that it was 'an affirmation of separateness'.[37]
On the Venetian side, in contrast, it may be worth recording the
comment of a late-seventeenth-century British visitor that in the
Doge's Palace the beauty of the building was 'much prejudiced by
the beastliness of those that walk along and that leave their marks
behind them, as if this was rather a common house of office than
so noble a palace'.[38]

---

[35]   An overview in Porter (1991); cf. Bremmer and Roodenburg (1991). Rudolf Braun of
the University of Zürich is writing a study of the dance in the early modern period from this
point of view.
[36]   Overview in Burke (1987); on clothes, Roche (1989); on humour, Thomas (1977).
[37]   Spierenburg (1981); Schama (1987), 380.
[38]   Burnet (1686), 130.

Language too ought to have a place in a study of seventeenth-century elites. The increasing use of French among the regent class in Amsterdam in the seventeenth century – like the use of French by Russian nobles in the age of Tolstoy – was, among other things, a symbolic expression of the distinction between the elite and ordinary people, which ought to be added to the inventory of the signs of their 'aristocratization' discussed below (pp. 129ff).[39]

In Venice, on the other hand, it is the continuing attachment of the patricians to the local dialect as late as the eighteenth century, at least in some social contexts, which most deserves emphasis. Venetian, and not standard Italian, was the language used in courts of law, and it remained the language of poetry (as in the case of the lyrics of Antonio Ottobon*). In these cases too we might explain the phenomenon as an affirmation of separateness, of the desire of Venetians not to lose their collective identity.[40] It is for this reason that the names of the Venetian patricians are given in their dialect form (Lunardo, for example, rather than Leonardo, or Zuan rather than Giovanni).

Another topic which deserves to be discussed in more detail is that of changing forms of 'sociability', as the French historian Maurice Agulhon calls it, especially the various forms of voluntary association, from the literary to the military, to which members of the two elites belonged.[41] In the case of Venice, there were the religious fraternities, the dramatic societies (p. 115 below) and the academies (of which more than sixty were founded in the seventeenth century alone, some of them under the protection of members of the elite such as Angelo Morosini* and Sebastiano Soranzo*). In Amsterdam one should mention not only the civic militia, the famous *schutterij*, but also the chambers of rhetoric, notably De Egelantier, whose members in the early seventeenth century were drawn from such patrician families as Corver, Hooft, Huydecoper, Pauw, Reael and Reynst.[42]

I continue to suspect that these institutions exemplify the importance of what Johan Huizinga called the 'play element in culture',

---

[39]   Willem Frijhoff promises a study of this topic.
[40]   Vianello (1957). For poetry in Venetian dialect, Dazzi (1956).
[41]   Agulhon (1968), Introduction.
[42]   On the militia, Haverkamp-Begemann (1982), 37f; on De Egelantier, Kalff (1906–12), vol. 4, 60.

in the sense that they were essentially male clubs in which sociability and the sense of 'festive community' – fortified by ritualized
eating and drinking, and smoking – was at least as important as
the official purpose of the association, whether this happened to be
writing poems and plays or defending the city.[43] The network of
such clubs in a city such as Amsterdam would make a good subject
for a thesis. Despite the increasing number of studies published on
these two cities and their elites in the last twenty years, much still
remains to be done. I hope that the republication of this essay may
serve to encourage further research.

The original text has been revised for this edition, and recent
research has been incorporated in the notes as well as in the
bibliography.

Cambridge, June 1993

---

[43] Huizinga (1938); on drink and sociability, Douglas (1988); on festive community,
Schama (1987), 178ff; on male associations, Völger and Welck (1990).

Abbreviations

ASV	Archivio di Stato, Venice
BCV	Biblioteca Correr, Venice
BL	British Library
BMV	Biblioteca Marciana, Venice
CS	Collaterale Successie (Registers of Collateral Succession in GA)
EIP	Esame Istorico Politico (anonymous MS in BCV, Gradenigo 15)
GA	Gemeente Archief, Amsterdam
K	Dutch pamphlets, cited by their number in Knuttel's catalogue
NNBW	*Nieuw Nederlands Biografische Woordenboek*, ed. P. C. Molhuysen et al., 10 vols, Leiden 1911–37
RA	'Relazione dell'anonimo', in *Curiosità di storia veneziana*, ed. P. Molmenti, Bologna 1919, 359–438
SV	*Studi Veneziani* (formerly *Bollettino di storia della società e dello stato veneziano*)
VOC	Vereenigde Oost-Indische Compagnie (Dutch East India Company)
WIC	West-Indische Compagnie (Dutch West India Company)

1

The Study of Elites

This book is an essay in comparative social history.[1] It is only in the last generation, more particularly in France, the USA and Great Britain, that social history has become a serious independent discipline. It is becoming as rigorous in its methods as economic history, after a long period in which it had been the preserve of amateurs and antiquarians, who collected (as one reviewer, John Wilson Croker, wrote – cruelly but correctly – of the famous third chapter in Macaulay's *History of England*) no more than an 'old curiosity shop' of miscellaneous information. The fault was partly in the negative conception of social history current until quite recently, a conception expressed in George Macaulay Trevelyan's notorious definition of it as 'history with the politics left out'.[2]

The newer social history, or 'societal history' as it is sometimes called, might be defined more positively as the study of social change in specific communities, where 'social change' means change in the social structure, the groups which make up society. The newer social historians attempt to combine the attention to detail and the interest in change over time characteristic of the traditional historian with the social scientist's interest in problems, and so in comparisons. They tend to focus on the history of particular social groups in specific regions over a generation, a

[1] See above, p. xii, and Redlich (1958).
[2] Trevelyan (1942), vii.

century or even longer. Among the examples from the 1950s and 1960s that spring to mind are those of Elinor Barber on the bourgeoisie in eighteenth-century France; Hans Rosenberg on aristocrats and bureaucrats in Prussia; Edward Thompson on the English working class in the early nineteenth century; Lawrence Stone on the English aristocracy between 1558 and 1641; Marc Raeff on the nobility of eighteenth-century Russia; and Emmanuel Le Roy Ladurie on the peasants of Languedoc in the sixteenth and seventeenth centuries.

The historian of aristocracies, at least, can learn something from the sociological study of elites, defined throughout this book as groups high on three criteria: status, power and wealth.[3] The dominant figure in the sociological study of elites was the Italian Vilfredo Pareto, who wrote at the beginning of this century. Pareto raided history for his own purposes; historians might well make use of him for theirs.

Like that of other 'functionalists', as supporters of this approach are often called, Pareto's model of society was one of a 'system' of parts or particles interacting to produce what he called 'social equilibrium'. Without necessarily committing themselves to a grand general theory, or taking the analogy with engineering too seriously, social historians may find it useful to look at the interaction of economic, political and cultural factors in the life of a social group. Pareto argued that an important mechanism of social equilibrium was what he called the 'circulation of elites'. Among the types of elites he distinguished were 'lions' and 'foxes', terms he borrowed from Machiavelli to refer to military and political groups, and, in the economic field, 'rentiers' and 'speculators'. Rentiers are essentially men on fixed incomes, while speculators (perhaps better translated as 'entrepreneurs') pursue profit and take more risks.

True to his emphasis on the relations between the parts of the social system, Pareto used these terms to refer not only to the economic basis of the two elites but to their intellectual and psychological make-up. Entrepreneurs are active, imaginative, interested in innovation, 'speculators' in the philosophical as well as

---

[3] G. Parry (1969) and J. Parry (1984) are lucid general introductions to elites and aristocracies.

in the economic sense of the term. Rentiers are passive, unimaginative, conservative. The distinction is not unlike Adam Smith's distinction between the 'merchant' and the 'gentleman' quoted in the epigraph to this volume, and Smith too is interested in the psychology or, as he puts it, the 'temper and disposition' of his two groups.

Unlike Smith, Pareto is not a supporter of the entrepreneur. He is neutral. He notes that periods of economic growth favour the entrepreneur, while periods of stagnation or contraction favour the rentier. However, he argues that these two elites each have a social function: one to advance change, and the other to resist it. Both functions are necessary. A society ruled by rentiers would stagnate; a society ruled by entrepreneurs would dissolve into chaos. What is needed is a judicious balance between the two. The elites follow their own interests and do not aim at social equilibrium, but social equilibrium results from their interaction. Each group has conscious aims which affect society, but the two groups are not conscious of their social functions – in other words the unintended consequences of their deliberate actions.[4]

Pareto is brilliant and stimulating, but he operates at such a general level that a historian may well feel somewhat lost. As a corrective to such 'grand theory', the American sociologist C. Wright Mills wrote *The Power Elite* (1956) and so revived the study of the subject. In this book, written with passion and imagination, Mills studied the political, business and military hierarchies in the USA at the time of the Korean war and emphasized that they 'interlocked'. He argued that a 'compact and powerful' elite had come to dominate America, that businessmen and generals influenced key political decisions and that this was a bad thing. Mills had a good deal to say about the style of life and the attitudes of the elite, and I have tried to emulate him in this respect. However, the controversy which his book raised showed the difficulty of testing the elite theory empirically, and especially of showing that a given elite forms a cohesive group.

The fundamental problems of method have been raised lucidly and elegantly by an American political scientist, Robert Dahl. He

---

[4] Pareto (1916), paras 2233ff.

defines a 'ruling elite' as a minority whose preferences regularly prevail in cases of conflict over key political issues. The implication of this definition is that one needs (i) a well-defined minority, (ii) conflict situations and (iii) evidence that the minority regularly prevails, before one can use the term 'ruling elite' at all.[5] This is perhaps to minimize the power of an elite to smother potential conflict – for example, by withholding crucial information, or by excluding certain issues from the political agenda – but it is a valuable reminder of the need for methodological rigour.[6]

Dahl's own solution to the problems of method he raised was to focus on the process of decision-making in a single city, New Haven. From 1784 to 1842, he argued, 'social status, education, wealth and political influence were united in the same hands', in a group he called 'the patricians', men of established New Haven families who were lawyers by profession. In the mid nineteenth century the industrialization of America promoted social change and the patricians were replaced by 'the entrepreneurs', industrialists who had wealth and gained power but lacked high status. As for the twentieth century, Dahl concluded that 'oligarchy' had been replaced by 'pluralism', in other words that there is not very much overlap between wealth, status and power, although 'economic notables' and 'social notables' in New Haven may influence specific political decisions.[7]

The historian of seventeenth-century Europe can learn something from each of these writers, and indeed from other recent work on elites. Mills and Dahl both suggest that one does well to study the overlap between men of wealth, men of status and men of power. From Pareto one can borrow the concepts of 'rentier', 'entrepreneur', 'social system' and 'social function'.

Dahl's example also suggested that research on elites might be more manageable if a city rather than a nation was made the focus of attention. In seventeenth-century Europe there were not many cities politically independent enough for this approach to be useful, but Venice and Amsterdam fall into this category. There were certain obvious similarities between them of which contempor-

---

[5] Dahl (1958).
[6] Bachrach and Baratz (1962).
[7] Dahl (1961).

aries were well aware, like travellers since.[8] In 1567, for instance, the Tuscan Ludovico Guicciardini called Amsterdam 'the Venice of the North'. In 1600 a French visitor, the Duc de Rohan, commented that Amsterdam was so like Venice that 'I find nothing in one which has not close parallels in the other.' In 1618 the Venetian envoy A. Donà called Amsterdam 'the image of Venice in the days when it was rising' (*l'immagine della già nascente Venezia*). In 1650 an Amsterdam pamphleteer accused the powerful Bicker family of wanting to take over the Republic and create another Venice.[9]

There were of course connections of various kinds between the two republics in this period, but this subject will not be discussed here, any more than the uses of the Venetian model of government in the Netherlands or vice versa.[10] The focus will be on comparison, in the sense of a systematic study of both similarities and differences. Seventeenth-century Amsterdam and Venice were remarkably similar in a number of respects. In a Europe mainly composed of monarchies each was the greatest city of a republic.[11] The doge was a kind of constitutional monarch, but his powers were severely limited, while the Dutch Stadholder was a kind of doge, a survival into republican times of the nobles who governed provinces on behalf of a prince such as Philip II. In a Europe where the ruling class still tended to identify with fighters the patricians of Venice and Amsterdam were predominantly civilian. In Pareto's terms, they were foxes in a world of lions. In a Europe whose governing elites usually despised trade Amsterdam and Venice stood out as places where, at least in the early seventeenth century, trade and politics could be combined with success. The values of the two groups included a stress on tolerance and thrift, two qualities not usually prized by seventeenth-century leaders. In a Europe whose ruling classes tended to spend most of their time on their country estates the patricians of Venice and Amsterdam lived mainly in town. The economic basis, the ethos and the style of life of the two groups changed in a similar way in the course of the

---

[8]   Notably Havard (1876).
[9]   Rohan (1661), vol. 2, 359; Blok (1909), 112; K. 6773, 5–6.
[10] Jonge (1852); Haitsma Mulier (1980); Mastellone (1983).
[11] Durand (1973).

century; the reverse of nineteenth-century New Haven, they began as entrepreneurs and ended as rentiers.

There were also striking differences between the two groups. The Venetian elite was one of noblemen, the Amsterdam elite one of commoners. The Venetians were Catholic, the Amsterdammers mainly Protestant. In Amsterdam the nuclear family was the focus of loyalty, in Venice the extended family. Both similarities and differences suggest that systematic comparison might be worthwhile, since this approach draws the attention of the historian to what contemporaries usually do not see, notably, the connections between different parts of their culture.

For example, later chapters will argue that the Venetian elite, as a nobility, was more oriented towards the family and less towards individual achievement than the bourgeois Amsterdammers. The Venetians were more concerned with display, especially family display, while Amsterdammers set a higher value on frugality, a bourgeois virtue reinforced by their Calvinism. Children brought up in a nuclear family, as in Amsterdam, were more likely to develop a need to achieve than were Venetian noble children, reared in an extended family. Venetians, trained in an old university, Padua, and living in a city with a glorious past, were more likely to prize the old than were Amsterdammers, trained in new institutions like the Athenaeum and Leiden University, and living in a fairly new and rapidly expanding city. Again, the fact that in Venice it was common for only one brother per generation to marry cannot be understood without reference to the system of which this social convention formed a part: the need for birth control so as not to impoverish the family, the fact that brothers tended to live together in the family palace so that a bachelor was not isolated and the importance of career opportunities for the celibate in the church and in the navy (many naval officers married late or not at all).

Comparative history also helps one to see what is not there. For instance, the lack in the Veneto of societies of noblemen concerned with the reform of agriculture becomes all the more striking when we think of the importance of such societies in England, France, Tuscany and elsewhere in the eighteenth century (below, p. 61). The fact that Venice did not grow in the period and that Venetians did not form joint-stock companies looks more significant when one thinks of the rapid growth of Amsterdam and the importance of the Dutch East India Company, the VOC. Conversely, the example of Venice, where the patricians of the city dominated the *terraferma* (the north Italian mainland, including the areas around the cities of Padua, Vicenza, Verona, Bergamo and Brescia), encourages us to ask why the Amsterdammers did not invest more heavily in land and suggests that it might be illuminating to look at Amsterdam's relation to the province of Holland – as opposed to the Dutch Republic as a whole, the 'United Provinces' as people called them – in terms of a city-state dominating the territory round about it.[12]

The comparative approach comes naturally to an outsider, whereas the history of Amsterdam and Venice has been written for the most part by their citizens (often by descendants of the patricians). Two outstanding examples are Pompeo Molmenti's *History of Venice in Private Life* (1879) and Johan Elias's *The Aldermen of Amsterdam* (1903–5). Each was the life-work of its author. Molmenti was concerned with social history, paying particular attention to the patricians, and if he did not altogether escape the defects of the 'old curiosity shop' approach to social history, he was a pioneer in his field. As for Elias, he was a political historian who collected information about the genealogy, offices and wealth of every member of the Town Council; his work is in fact a treasury of under-analysed data. Both men wrote of 'their' cities with great affection so that it is appropriate that a square in Venice should bear Molmenti's name today. An outsider cannot hope to emulate the virtues of these men. A different approach may at least prevent him or her from carrying water to the Grand Canal, or, for that matter, to the Amstel.

The remaining chapters will raise and attempt to answer the following questions.

What is the structure of the elite in Amsterdam and Venice? How is it recruited? Is it an 'estate' or a 'class'?
What are its political functions? To what extent does it rule, over whom and by what means?

---

[12] Since the first edition of this book, this suggestion, argued by Dillen (1964), has been supported by Braudel (1979), 145ff, and criticized by Israel (1989), 415.

What is its economic base? Is it relatively rich or poor and if rich,
   where does its wealth come from?
What is its style of life?
How is it trained?
What are its most important attitudes and values?
To what extent and in what ways does it patronize the arts?
How and why does the group change during the period?

The period with which the book is concerned is a long seventeenth century running from about 1580 to about 1720. It is
convenient to begin around 1580, although the revolt of the
Netherlands against Spain had begun in 1572, because the Town
Council of Amsterdam was almost completely replaced in 1578
(the famous *Alteratie*), while in Venice there were important constitutional changes in 1582, leading to a decline in the power of
the Council of Ten and its 'junta'. The importance of the changes
in both cities is controversial, as will be seen below (pp. 36, 43),
but it remains difficult to find better starting-points.[13] It is convenient to end the seventeenth century around 1720 because it was in
the early eighteenth century that the two groups ceased to be
involved in foreign wars, when the Dutch Republic made the
Treaty of Utrecht with the French (1713) and the Venetians made
the Treaty of Passarowitz with the Turks (1718). There is no other
obvious moment to stop till the 1790s, when Napoleon finally put
an end to both these republican regimes.

The approach adopted in this book is prosopographical. That
is, an attempt is made to answer the eight questions listed above by
studying collective biography, the biography of 563 men. For
Venice the group selected for study was the doges and *procuratori
di San Marco*, 244 men in all; for Amsterdam it was the 319
burgomasters and members of the Town Council. In each case the
dates chosen were 1578–1719 inclusive. Members of these groups
who figure in the text will henceforth be marked by an asterisk.

The limitations and dangers of the prosopographical approach
have been described by one of its leading English practitioners,
Professor Lawrence Stone, and his warnings certainly apply to the
study of Venice and Amsterdam in the seventeenth century.[14]

---

13   Roorda (1964); Dudok van Heel (1991b); Lowry (1971).
14   Stone (1971); cf. Burke (1993b).

The most obvious limitation is the one of deficiencies in the data. In the case of the 563 men studied below it has usually been possible to discover something about their families, wealth and political careers, but it is much harder to find out about their taste in painting or their conception of God. A few individuals in each city have left abundant evidence, including letters, memoirs and autobiographies, making possible biographies of Marcantonio Barbaro,* for example, Nicolò Contarini,* Lunardo Donà,* Agostino Nani,* Coenraed van Beuningen,* Joan Blaeu,* Joan and Gerrit Corver,* Cornelis P. Hooft,* Jacob van Neck* and Nicolaes Witsen.*[15] The Donà, Dolfin, Elias and Trip families, who all contributed members to the elite, have also been the object of monographs.[16]

There is a larger group of patricians for whose attitudes the evidence is thinner, and a larger group still about whom there are only a few clues or no clues at all. The obvious danger here is the one about which Stone warns intending prosopographers: of treating the sample about whom there is reliable information as a random sample of the whole population being studied, when it is not. The analysis will usually start from well-known examples, like the eleven men listed above, but without assuming that they were typical of the rest.

In the case of art patronage in Amsterdam, there are especially good reasons for supposing that the minority of whose patronage we are well informed – Andries de Graeff,* for instance, or Joan Huydecoper* – were not typical of the majority of their colleagues in office. In other words, even using the methods of collective biography, it is not possible to generalize on an absolutely firm basis. However, to talk about the group without looking at some of its members one by one is to generalize without a basis at all.

Throughout this study the two elites will be described as 'patricians'. The term *patricii* was coined in ancient Rome to refer to the children of the early senators, or *patres*, and so to the members of certain old families. It was revived by humanists in the fifteenth

[15] Yriarte (1885); Cozzi (1958); Seneca (1959); F. Nani Mocenigo (1894); Roldanus (1931); Koeman (1970); Porta (1975); H. A. E. van Gelder (1918); Terpstra (1960); Gebhard (1881).
[16] Davis (1975); Dolfin (1924); J. E. Elias (1937); P. W. Klein (1965).

century and applied to urban aristocracies such as those of
Nuremberg and Venice, and the term has tended to be used in
that sense ever since, though with different shades of meaning.
For the author of one comparative study, it refers to upper-class
office-holders of old family in a regime in which there are also
non-patricians in office.[17]

In Venice in the seventeenth century the term *patrizii* was used
of noblemen in general, while in Amsterdam – despite the elite's
identification with ancient Romans – it was not used at all. It
remains convenient to use the term 'patrician' in this book to refer
to the 563 men who are its subject. How the 563 were chosen will
be discussed in the next chapter.

[17]   Notestein (1968); contrast Cowan (1986), ch. 1.

2

Structure

The greatest problem to be faced in making this study is that of identifying the two elites.[1] However rigorous one may try to be in the analysis of collective biographies, the biographies have to be chosen in the first place on the basis of more impressionistic evidence. It is therefore necessary to attempt an answer to the question, what groups had status, power and wealth in Venice and Amsterdam in the seventeenth century? The essential point to make is that Venice was an 'estate society', while Amsterdam was a 'class society' (much more unusual in seventeenth-century Europe). In other words Venice was divided into formally defined status groups, and power and wealth tended to follow status. In Amsterdam, by contrast, status groups were defined informally, so that status tended to follow wealth and power.[2]

In Venice the traditional division of society into three estates – the clergy, the nobility and the rest – was still taken seriously enough to be a social fact. The clergy can be dealt with briefly. As in other parts of Catholic Europe, there was an important distinction between high-status upper clergy – the patriarch, the bishops of the *terraferma* and the *primicerio*, or dean of the Church of San Marco – and low-status lower clergy, such as parish priests and

[1]   No references will be given for biographical material drawn from 'Il Barbaro', Capellari and J. E. Elias (1903–5).
[2]   Mousnier (1969), chs 1, 3.

friars. The upper clergy were usually noblemen, while the lower clergy were usually members of the third estate.

The second estate was a legally defined high-status group. Nobles were those men, women and children whose names were entered in the *libro d'oro*, the golden book. In 1580 this meant, with very few exceptions, that they were descended from people considered noble in 1297 (the date of the notorious *Serrata*, or 'closing' of the patriciate). Noblemen over the age of twenty-five were eligible for political office. In 1594 there were 1,967 male nobles over the age of twenty-five, omitting honorary nobles like the Este family of Ferrara.[3] In the mid seventeenth century, when the government was in financial difficulties, it became possible for families to buy their way into the nobility (for 100,000 ducats a time), but in spite of the 'aggregation' of 100 new families by this means, in 1719 there were only 1,703 male nobles over twenty-five.[4] They were thus a tiny minority of the population of Venice, which in 1720 as in 1580 was about 140,000.[5]

Within this estate there were gradations of status. Old families were considered more honourable than new ones, and most honourable were the twenty-four 'old families' (*case vecchie*) who claimed to have been noble and Venetian before 800. However, if processions can be seen in Venice as elsewhere in early modern Europe as materializations of the social structure – which is why struggles over precedence were conducted in such deadly earnest – then it is clear that the fundamental distinction between one nobleman and another from the point of view of status was the holding of office. First came the doge, a kind of constitutional monarch, a head of state unable to take political initiative; then the *procuratori di San Marco*, who were something like life peers; and next the holders of other important political offices. Status and power were closely associated in Venice, and to power we must now turn.

In theory, Venice was governed by a council, the Greater Council (*Maggior Consiglio*), which included all male nobles over twenty-five together with a few under that age. In that sense, status

[3]   BCV, MS Donà 225.
[4]   BCV, MS Cicogna 913.
[5]   Beltrami (1954), 38.

and power coincided. Of course an assembly of some two thousand members was much too big to exercise effective power, and its main function was to appoint some of its members to office. There was also an upper house, or Senate, which made some important appointments, and could sometimes put pressure on the Greater Council, but even the Senate, with about two hundred members, was too large for effective decision-making. To find out who exercised power in Venice it is necessary to look at the holders of key offices. It has been calculated that there were about eight hundred offices in the seventeenth century, and most of them rotated rapidly, changing hands every six months, or eight months, or every year, or every three years.[6] The student of Venetian politics therefore needs to identify the key offices and the men who regularly held them. How does one know a man was powerful? Because he held key offices.

How does one know that certain offices were key offices? Because powerful men tended to hold them. The danger of circularity will be obvious. It is difficult for a historian to improve on the opinion of contemporaries, who generally considered that important office included appointments to be an ambassador, to govern major cities of the *terraferma*, to be *savio*, to be a member of the Council of Ten or to hold a high naval post. However, concentration on the holders of important offices runs the risk of omitting the unofficial leaders, the grey eminences who had more power than their offices warranted. Domenico Molin, brother of Doge Francesco Molin,* was said to be such a man.

After status and power, the third hierarchy to investigate is that of wealth, which Venetians calculated in ducats (so called because the head of the doge, or *dux,* appeared on the coins). It is probably best not to try to convert Venetian ducats into modern currencies, but to compare rich and poor within Venice instead. In order to assess the significance of the figures which follow, the reader may like to bear in mind that in the late sixteenth century a journeyman mason earned about 50 ducats a year.

A systematic investigation of the wealth of Venetians was made by the government for tax purposes in 1581, 1661 and 1711.[7] The

[6] Davis (1962), 22.
[7] Canal (1908).

historian has reason to be grateful that in Venice, unlike most parts of Europe, the nobility was subject to taxation. In 1581, according to the tax records, fifty-nine heads of households declared an annual income from land and houses of more than 2,000 ducats a year. All were nobles but three: dal Basso, di Mutti and della Vecchia. In 1711 seventy heads of household declared 6,000 ducats or more annual income; all were noble but one (Donado Pozzi), though eleven more were recently 'aggregated' nobles (Bonfadini, Bressa, Carminati, Correggio, Fini, Labia, Minelli, Papafava, Piovene, Vidman and Zenobio).

Unfortunately for us, the tax returns give no information about any wealth which was not invested in land or houses. However, virtually all rich landowners were noble, though many nobles were not rich men. In Venice, as in parts of France, Spain, Poland or Japan, the poor noble was a well-known phenomenon at this time. Wealth was linked to status and power because some offices, like ambassadorships, involved their holders in so much expense that they had to be rich men to accept them; because rich commoners, from the mid seventeenth century onwards, were able to buy their way into the nobility; and because some nobles were able to buy the high-status appointments of *procuratori di San Marco*. In short, there was enough overlap between status, power and wealth for the historian to talk about a relatively unified elite.

'Not all the stars of the Milky Way need to be known by the astrologers, but only the great ones which have influence on this sublunary world,' remarked a contemporary student of Venetian politics.[8] As a substantial sample of these influential men, I have chosen to concentrate, throughout this study, on the twenty-five doges of the period and on the *procuratori di San Marco*, henceforth referred to as 'proctors'. Proctors looked after the Church of San Marco and administered certain charities. They went round Venice distributing alms and looked after minors and the property of people who died intestate. They came next to the doge in official status, and doges were supposed to be chosen from among them (though seven doges in the period were not). The proctors were exceptions to the rapid turnover of office in Venice. They were

[8]   RA, 401.

appointed for life by the Greater Council and they were senators *ex officio*.

There were nine 'ordinary' proctors, but 'extraordinary' appointments could be made, and were indeed often made for money, usually from 20,000 to 25,000 ducats. About a third of the appointments in the period were extraordinary ones. There were 237 proctors in this period, and the addition of the 7 doges who were not proctors brings the group to be studied to 244. Not all powerful Venetians were proctors, but most proctors were or had been powerful. About three-quarters of them had held high office before appointment, and after appointment their position as permanent senators gave them an opportunity to be influential. Not all rich Venetians were proctors, but the proctors were among the richest men in Venice. In 1581 half the proctors, 9 out of 18, had an income of 2,000 ducats a year or more from houses and land, in other words belonged to the richest 60 households in the city. In 1711 20 out of 38 proctors declared 6,000 ducats a year or more, so that over half came from the richest 70 households. Conversely, about 30 per cent of the richest heads of households were proctors.

The increase in the numbers of these officials between 1581 and 1711 shows how in Venice, as in England in the seventeenth century, the financial needs of the government led to an 'inflation of honours'. It may be significant that the price of a proctorship was only about a quarter of what it cost a new family to join the Venetian nobility. The great distinction in Venice was between those who were noble and those who were not.

In Amsterdam the traditional division of society into three estates was ceasing to be useful. Where the Catholic clergy had been seen as a separate estate, the Protestant clergy were regarded as a group of professional men not unlike lawyers and doctors. As for the second estate, Dutch noblemen tended to be found at The Hague (at the court of the stadholder, when there was one) or in the country on their own lands.

The term 'estate' continued to be used by contemporaries, but it changed its meaning as it was applied to different groups within the third estate. Thus C. P. Hooft* in the early seventeenth century referred to people 'of middle or still lower estate' (*van* *middelbaren ofte noch lageren staet*) as opposed to 'the richest, most honourable and most notable people' (*de rijcksten, eerbaersten ende notabelsten personen*).[9] Again, a pamphlet published in Amsterdam in 1662 expressed shock at merchants and shopkeepers who forget themselves and climb above their estate (*boven sijnen staet treden*), though the writer had to admit that in Amsterdam merchants included many people of 'power and wealth' (*macht en middelen*).[10]

There was clearly a need for a new term to characterize differences in social status in a new way, and the word 'class' was just beginning to come into use in this sense. In the sixteenth century the Latin word *classis* was used of religious groups in the presbyterian system of church government. In the early seventeenth century it was used of 'classes' of pupils. In the late seventeenth century it was used about groups paying different amounts of tax. It seems to have been the philosopher Baruch Spinoza who first used the term in a more general way to refer to a social group. His *Ethics* (1678) contains the statement – in Latin – that men transfer the love or hate they feel towards an individual stranger to 'the whole class or nation whereto he belongs'.[11]

Curiously enough, an early use of the term 'class' in English also has as its context the social structure of the Dutch Republic. Sir William Temple, who served as ambassador to the United Provinces, wrote an account of that country in which he divided the people into five 'classes' – peasants, sailors, merchants, rentiers and gentlemen.[12] It seems useful to take over this word and to describe the Amsterdam elite as an 'upper class', implying that social status was not defined in legal terms but that in practice men of power and wealth were accorded high status by their fellows.[13] This state of affairs was one which shocked some foreign observers. In 1586 a member of the circle of the Earl of Leicester, who had been sent to the Netherlands by Queen Elizabeth, described the Dutch regent class with evident contempt as 'the sovereign lords millers and cheesemen' (one member of the Amsterdam

---

[9]   C. P. Hooft (1871–1925), vol. 1, 109, 168.
[10] K.8670, 2.
[11] Quoted in Ossowski (1957), 122n.
[12] Temple (1673), 97.
[13] Cf. Schöffer (1968).

Town Council at this time, B. Appelman,* was indeed a dealer in cheese).[14]

It remains to see to what extent power and wealth overlapped in Amsterdam. The men of power are easier to identify than in Venice, because there were fewer offices and they rotated less often. Amsterdam had a Town Council (*vroedschap*) with 36 councillors (*raadslieden*) appointed for life. There was also a sheriff (*schout*), 9 magistrates (*schepenen*) and 4 burgomasters, often but not always members of the Council. The burgomasters were independent of the Council, which was unusual for Dutch towns and a clue to the political influence of Amsterdam.[15] These burgomasters were appointed by the ex-burgomasters and ex-magistrates for a year, but one of the 4 served a second term to ensure continuity. Burgomasters and Council together come to 319 men, the 'power elite' of Amsterdam in the period.

The best sources for the wealth of Amsterdammers as of Venetians are the investigations made for tax purposes. There were tax assessments in 1585, 1631 and 1674. The *kohier* (assessment) of 1585 shows that the richest and the second-richest men in Amsterdam were burgomasters and that about half the Council were among the richest 65 households.[16] According to the *kohier* of 1631, 24 heads of households were worth 200,000 florins or more (taxation was levied on property, not income). Six of these 24 were members of the Council (and 7 of the remaining 18 were women or children).[17] According to the *kohier* of 1674, 81 heads of households were worth 200,000 florins or more; 15 of these were members of the Council, 4 were future members (and 19 of the remainder were women or children).[18]

There were a few rich men in Amsterdam who never entered the Council, like D. Alewijn, G. Bartolotti and B. Coymans (three examples taken from the 1631 *kohier*), but in these cases their relatives by blood or marriage did. The Jewish businessmen of the city are conspicuously absent. All the same, we may conclude that wealth, status and power overlapped to an unusual extent in

[14] Wilson (1970), 23.
[15] Fruin (1889).
[16] Dillen (1941).
[17] Frederiks and Frederiks (1890).
[18] GA, Kohier 1674.

Amsterdam at this time and that it is possible to study the 319 burgomasters and councillors as a unified elite.

An obvious – and important – question to ask about elites is how they are recruited. Who chose them? From whom were they chosen? On what criteria?

In Venice proctors were elected by the Greater Council. But how did certain individuals come to be elected? Gasparo Contarini's famous sixteenth-century description of the Venetian constitution declares that men are elected proctors who have held many offices and are of obvious merit (*una riguardevole bontà*).[19] Some seventeenth-century writers were more cynical. They suggested that what mattered was money, or family connections (*parentele*) or patronage (*amicitia, adherenze*), in this case presumably the group of clients voting for their patron rather than the patron getting a job for one of his clients. This was the 'tripod' on which political success in Venice was based.[20] Family and patronage were crucial in that central informal political institution of Venice, the *broglio*, the regular open-air meetings of noblemen at San Marco or the Rialto where the intriguing and bargaining went on before the formal elections in the Greater Council. 'The man with important relatives is honoured and he who is provided with friends is provided with offices.'[21]

It is not easy to place these different factors in order of importance. Take money, for example. A third of the proctors bought their offices. This does not prove that they would not have been elected anyway, although extraordinary proctors tended to have held fewer important offices than ordinary ones. To become a proctor, however, it was a great help to have been an ambassador, and only a man of wealth could afford this, given the expenses involved (below, p. 76). Again, to get one's foot on a bottom rung of the ladder of office it was a help to have been to university, and that too cost money. Even 'ordinary' proctors needed wealth.

As for family, a few statistics show its importance clearly. Of the 244 members of the Venetian elite, 42 were the sons of doges or proctors; 30, the brothers of doges or proctors; 18, the grandsons; 18, the sons-in-law; 12, the nephews. These figures confirm

---

[19]   G. Contarini (1543), fo. 58r.
[20]   EIP.
[21]   Relatione 1, fo. 77v.

what contemporaries point out, that there was a small number of wealthy and powerful families within the Venetian nobility, the 'princes of the blood' as they were sometimes called.[22] A notorious example is that of the Corner family (branch of San Maurizio), who were known as 'the Medici of Venice'.[23] Members of these families had a better chance of election to office from the time they ran for the junior post of *savio agl'ordini* down to the time they tried to become proctors.

According to a French observer, the Benedictine Camille Freschot, the power of these families was exercised through the lesser nobles, 'who are entirely theirs' (*qui sont entièrement à leur dévotion*).[24] Unfortunately, it is difficult to test this hypothesis. The numbers of votes for and against individual appointments was scrupulously recorded, but not the names of those who voted. Hence the historian can do little more than collect contemporary gossip. It was said, for example, that Alvise Priuli* was 'a great supporter of his clients' (*assai partigiano dei suoi clienti*), and that Marino Grimani* was elected doge because Lunardo Donà* persuaded his clients among the electors to vote for Grimani.[25]

The factor hardest to measure is of course talent. On this question, two contrary points need to be made. The first is that an able nobleman whose family was not wealthy or powerful did have a chance of reaching the top. Perhaps the most spectacular case in the period was that of Nicolò da Ponte,* who began as a poor noble from a minor family, made 150,000 ducats and finally surprised everyone by his election as doge at the age of about eighty-seven. Again, Nicolò Contarini* did not come from a very distinguished branch of his family, and in 1582 he declared an income of only 323 ducats; but he became doge in 1630 none the less. Lunardo Donà* was not a member of a powerful family and he declared an income of 326 ducats in 1582, but he was elected doge in 1606.

On the other hand, seventeenth-century writers sometimes remarked on the number of mediocrities in high office in Venice. One anonymous contemporary (whether a disappointed competi-

---

22 'Distinzioni', 18. Cf. Cozzi (1986).
23 Venier, 137.
24 Freschot (1709), vol. 1, 263.
25 EIP, 42; Mosto (1960), 314.

tor for office we do not know) said that gifted men might fail to become proctors because they had given offence, while some proctors 'made an impression by their robes and nothing more' (non fanno altra figura che quella della lor veste).[26] About 25 per cent of the proctors held no important office before buying their post. Alvise Barbarigo,* for example, described by one contemporary as 'without virtues and without vice, a man who does not speak in the Senate'; by another as 'a good senator and zealous in the public service, but without qualities which really stand out' (che spicchino di molto).[27] Of Daniele Bragadin* we learn that he does not hold office and, as far as voting is concerned, 'lets himself be carried along by the current'. But he was a rich man and became a proctor at the early age of thirty-three for 20,500 ducats.[28] Alessandro Contarini* was lieutenant-general to the great Francesco Morosini,* but was described as 'a majestic presence' (una maestosa presenza) with nothing inside, like an uninhabited palace.[29]

Not only mediocrity but inefficiency, corruption and even treason were charges made against some of the elite. Zuan Cappello,* capitano generale da mar (the supreme naval commander), was imprisoned for a time on a charge of dilatoriness, though he was eventually acquitted. Francesco Morosini,* who had the most glorious naval career of the century, was accused of keeping public money for himself. Zorzi Morosini,* another naval officer, was imprisoned on one occasion for maladministration, but went on to be capitano generale da mar all the same, and to be knighted by the Senate for his services. Zuan Pesaro* was tried for his failings as commander against papal forces in 1643, but he ended his life as doge. Zaccaria Sagredo* was deprived of his proctorship in 1630 for abandoning ground to the enemy; five years later he was holding the honourable appointment of podestà of Padua. Piero Venier* was imprisoned for challenging a superior officer, and again for leaving the Arsenal when officially on guard, yet he was elected proctor for merit, not money. Jacopo Soranzo* was de-

[26] RA, 401.
[27] EIP, 63; RA, 40.
[28] EIP, 67ff.
[29] EIP, 77ff.

prived of his proctorship in 1584 and banished on a charge of revealing state secrets, but he was freed two years later. Which was the miscarriage of justice, the accusation or the pardon? In all these cases the historian may well wonder whether a clique of powerful families could cover up the gravest faults of its members, or whether a powerful man was likely to be framed by his rivals. A contemporary writer suggested that Soranzo, for example, was the victim of envy.[30]

In Amsterdam the formal criteria for appointment to the Council were to be over twenty-five, a citizen and resident in Amsterdam for the previous seven years. Burgomasters had to be over forty. It was not too difficult to become a citizen in expanding Amsterdam. The population of the city was about 30,000 in 1590; about 90,000 in 1620; about 140,000 in 1640; and stabilized at about 200,000 from 1680 onwards.[31] One could become a *poorter*, or citizen, of Amsterdam in three ways: by birth, by marriage or by paying a fee – 8 florins in 1600, 50 florins in 1650. Over 7,000 new citizens were in fact admitted, at an increasing rate, in the thirty-five years from 1578 onwards.[32] A large number of people were thus eligible for the Amsterdam Council, though vacancies were filled by co-option.

As in Venice, family connections, patronage and wealth all mattered as well as ability. Of the 319 members of the Dutch elite, 91 were the sons of other members; 52 were sons-in-law; 44 were grandsons; 10 were brothers; and 9 were nephews. If an individual were councillor, certain close relatives of his (such as brother) were excluded automatically from the Council, but there were ways round this rule. The brothers Cornelis and Andries de Graeff* were a powerful force in Amsterdam politics in the early seventeenth century. Cornelis, the elder, was a councillor from 1639 to 1664. His brother was therefore excluded, and was elected councillor only in 1665, just after the death of Cornelis. However, Andries could and did become burgomaster before this time. From 1655 to 1662 one of the two was always a burgo-

---

[30] Molin, 124.
[31] Schraa (1954).
[32] Dillen (1929), xxxii.

master, and between them they were burgomasters no fewer than seventeen times. The brothers Andries and Cornelis Bicker* were in a similar situation. The elder, Andries, was councillor from 1622 to 1652 and burgomaster ten times. Cornelis was never a councillor, but he was three times burgomaster. In 1646 seven of the Bicker family held political office at once (minor offices included), possibly a record.[33] The Bicker and de Graeff families were closely allied by marriage. Two daughters of Jacob de Graeff* married two Bicker brothers, and Jacob's son Andries de Graeff* married Elisabeth Bicker.[34]

Patronage mattered too, at least on occasion. In his autobiography Nicolaes Witsen,* son of Cornelis Witsen,* tells us that he was appointed to the Council as a result of his friendship with the powerful burgomaster Gillis Valckenier,* and that he was not appointed a magistrate before 1673 because until 1672 the Valckenier faction was weaker than the opposing faction, led by the de Graeffs.[35]

All the same, there were considerable opportunities for new men to enter the Council, by 'new men' meaning people whose ancestors had not been burgomasters or councillors of Amsterdam themselves. At least fifteen of the elite were first-generation immigrants to Amsterdam and thirty-three were second-generation immigrants. This group of forty-eight includes eight burgomasters. Adriaen Cromhout,* for example, was born in Friesland and Louys Trip* was born in Dordrecht. C. Bambeeck,* A. Pater,* J. Poppen,* J. Munter,* C. van Teylingen* and A. Velters* were all the sons of immigrants to Amsterdam. It is a remarkable fact that of these forty-eight, only two came from the south. Yet a third of the population of Amsterdam in 1622 were first- or second-generation emigrants from the south. One might regard this as statistical confirmation of the view that Amsterdammers regarded these southerners with hostility – a hostility expressed in Bredero's famous play, *The Spanish Brabanter*.[36]

Of course to be new to Amsterdam did not necessarily mean that a man was new to the regent class. There were important links

[33] J. E. Elias (1923), 119.
[34] Ibid., 105.
[35] Witsen (1872), 43.
[36] Muller (1941), vol. 2, 369ff.

between the regents of Amsterdam and those of other cities. Adriaen Pauw,* for instance, was the son of a burgomaster of Gouda; Claes van Heemskerck* was the son of a burgomaster of Leiden; and Willem Dedel,* the only first-generation immigrant to enter the elite after 1672, was the son of a burgomaster of The Hague. However, it is not difficult to find burgomasters of Amsterdam whose ancestors had not been regents at all. Four famous examples are Jacob Poppen,* Frans Banningh Cocq,* Nicolaes Tulp* and Louys Trip,* and a look at their careers will help to show what opportunities were available in Amsterdam to the politically and socially ambitious.

Jacob Poppen* was the son of an immigrant to Amsterdam who found a job packing herrings. At the age of twenty-seven Jacob married Liefgen Wuytiers, daughter of a former councillor, and the same year he became lieutenant in the civic guard. Three years later he became regent of an almshouse, and in another three he was chosen as a councillor. He ended up a burgomaster.

Frans Banningh Cocq* was the son of an apothecary, an immigrant from Bremen who was said to have been a beggar. But his father married Lijsbeth Banningh, whose family were well represented in the Council in the fifteenth and sixteenth centuries. Frans himself took the name of Banningh, went to university, and when he was twenty-five married Maria Overlander, daughter of Volckert Overlander,* a rich merchant who had been on the Council for the last twenty years. A new man himself, Volckert Overlander* had married a Hooft, one of the most famous families of seventeenth-century Amsterdam. Four years after his marriage Frans Banningh Cocq* entered the Council. He was burgomaster four times, knighted by the King of France, became Heer van Purmerland (the estate came through his wife) and is now remembered as the patron of Rembrandt's *Night Watch*.[37]

Nicolaes Tulp* was the son of a cloth-merchant, and a doctor of medicine from Leiden. He entered the Council relatively early, at the age of twenty-nine, and was able to celebrate fifty years in it. His second marriage was to a daughter of one of the elite, but he had been a councillor eight years at that point. He was burgomaster four times, though he was sixty-one the first time (in

---

[37] Haverkamp-Begemann (1982).

contrast to the new man, Andries Bicker* had become burgomaster when he was forty-one, just over the minimum age).

Finally, Louys Trip* was much more of an outsider, since he was born in Dordrecht. But he was an extremely rich man, a seventeenth-century Krupp, in other words munitions manufacturer (his mother was a de Geer, one of the family who exploited the famous 'copper mountain' in Sweden). He had the favour of the Stadholder (later William III of England), who made him a councillor following his purge of 1672. He became a burgomaster two years later.

The example of Frans Banningh Cocq* illustrates the value to an ambitious family of a systematic marriage policy, while the example of Louys Trip* illustrates the opportunities afforded by political crises. In a similar way to Trip, a group of new men entered the Council in 1578, when supporters of the revolt against Spain took over the government of Amsterdam. Indeed, most of the men in office after the *Alteratie* were new men (the most obvious exceptions are Willem Baerdesen* and Jacob Banningh*) and one of the burgomasters, Adriaen Cromhout,* was, as has been said, an immigrant. His descendants were to be prominent in Amsterdam politics in the next generation.[38]

To sum up: a comparison between the recruitment of the elite in Amsterdam and Venice is complicated by the fact that in Amsterdam one is looking at one process, recruitment to the Council, while in Venice one is looking at two processes – recruitment to the proctorship and recruitment to lesser office. All the same, some major differences between the two cities stand out. One of them can best be expressed diagramatically.

In Venice there was a tightly defined group which was eligible to rule, the nobles, but a more loosely defined inner group who

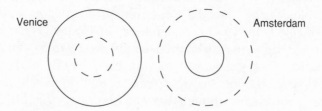

---

actually ruled. In Amsterdam there was a fairly loosely defined or open group which was eligible to rule, the citizens, but a much more closed inner group who actually ruled. In general, one may say that Venice was a relatively closed society, where for the first half of the period no new families were admitted to the nobility at all. Even after the ennoblements of the mid seventeenth century and after, proctors continued to be recruited from the same old families. The only exceptions are G. B. Albrizzi,* Vincenzo Fini* (the uncle), Vincenzo Fini* (the nephew), Ottavio Manin* and Antonio Ottobon.* Most of the new nobles were immigrants to Venice, usually from the mainland. They were able to buy their way in at the lower level, but not at the higher. Social mobility upwards was difficult in Venice, but so was downward mobility. A poor noble was a noble still. Members of the elite were concerned to help poor nobles. Silvestro Valier* left a fund for thirty noble families in decline, and Ferigo Contarini* was concerned with the foundation of an academy for the sons of poor nobles to receive a fitting education without payment. Amsterdam, on the other hand, was a more open society. Geographical mobility was possible, and an immigrant could become burgomaster. Social mobility upwards was possible. So was downward mobility – five of the elite went bankrupt and had to leave the Council: J. Hooghkamer,* J. van Neck,* J. Rijn* and D. Tholincx.* These examples also illustrate the link between wealth and power. In short, Venice was an estate society, as we have seen, while Amsterdam was a class society.

One might therefore expect the family to be more important in Venice, and the individual in Amsterdam. Statistics seem to bear this out. In Venice 244 elite members came from 66 families, an average of 3.7 each. Thirteen families had 6 or more members, led by 17 Contarini, 14 Corner and 13 Mocenigo. In Amsterdam 319 elite members came from 156 families, just over 2 members each. Six families had 6 or more members, led by 13 Bickers and 11 Backers. Family seems almost twice as important in Venice. But caution is necessary: 'family' did not mean the same thing in the two cities.

A striking feature of the Venetian nobility as a whole was how few surnames they had between them. In 1594 1,967 male nobles over the age of twenty-five had 139 surnames, about 14 individuals to each name. The most common names were Contarini (100 males), Morosini (68), Querini (54) and Malipiero and Priuli (52 each).[39] As certain Christian names were extremely popular in certain families – there were 7 Alvise Mocenigos in the elite in the period – the possibilities of confusion were great. Even contemporaries made mistakes; in 1607 the Greater Council was unsure which Andrea Vendramin was *podestà* of Chioggia. It is not surprising to find that Venetians tended to use patronymics, but even this did not always prevent confusion. The eighteenth-century antiquarian Capellari ascribes a diplomatic career to Doge Domenico di Giulio Contarini* which in fact belongs to another man with the same three names.

The problem is to discover what it meant to be a Contarini or a Morosini in seventeenth-century Venice. Historians tend to agree that the unit which mattered was not the group with the same surname (*famiglia*, best translated perhaps as 'clan') but the branch (*ramo*) or the house (*casa*), in other words the group which lived together in the same place and was usually named after its situation. Thus there were Corner members of the elite from five different branches – San Cassian, San Luca, San Maurizio, San Polo, San Samuele – named from the parishes in which they lived. Some branches of a clan might be rich, while others were miserably poor. One must not assume that members of the same clan voted the same way in the Greater Council and elsewhere. In the celebrated conflict between 'old' and 'young' in the later sixteenth century, for instance, Alberto Badoer supported the former while Ferigo Badoer supported the latter.[40]

All the same, I should like to argue that the solidarity of the clan has been somewhat underestimated. Members shared a coat of arms, a point which mattered in the seventeenth century. When a certain Girolamo Corner, from a minor branch of the clan, was condemned to death for treason in the early seventeenth century, the major branches offered 100,000 ducats, no small sum, to get him off, presumably to keep the clan name untarnished.[41] Some Correr wills prescribed that any woman in whom a given branch of the clan would become extinct must marry another Correr to

---

[39] BCV, MS Donà 225, MS Cicogna 913.
[40] Cozzi (1958), 6n.
[41] Mosto (1960), 358.
[42] Litta (1819), vol. 2, s.v. 'Correr'.

keep the wealth within the clan.[42] There is no doubt that some branches of major clans were aware of their close relationship to certain other branches, and this fact is likely to have made for solidarity between them.

The crucial question, from our point of view, is whether – other things being equal – a Venetian nobleman is more likely to have voted for another nobleman of the same surname in elections to office. This question cannot be answered directly, but it is suggestive that there were five Contarini doges during the period, from different branches. That is, they formed less than 5 per cent of the nobility but 25 per cent of the doges. An anonymous writer of the mid seventeenth century discusses the leading figures in Venetian politics and their assets, and emphasizes the support that their relatives give to certain members of the Contarini, Zustinian, Mocenigo and Morosini families – among the biggest surname groups of all. He writes of Girolamo Zustinian, for example, that 'as far as public elections are concerned, he depends on the "ringleaders" [caporioni] of the Zustinian family', a phrase which can hardly refer to one branch alone.[43] It is also interesting to learn that a meeting of all Contarini patricians over the age of forty took place in the Doge's Palace in 1682.

In private life the branch was certainly the unit, and its organization merits further description. It was not a nuclear family. Characteristically it was a group of brothers living in a palace with their wives and children. When a nobleman married, he would tend to bring his wife to the palace, the building which symbolized the branch and held it together. Noblemen in their wills exhort their sons not to split up to form more branches; Antonio Grimani* even told his sons to keep a common kitchen and a common table.[44] It is difficult to be precise about the average size of the branch or house. A list of 1714 mentions 216 noble families, 667 houses (case) and 2,851 males.[45] This would mean an average of just over 4 males to a branch. Presumably there would be as many women: unmarried girls living at home, and wives of the men. And of course the household would include servants too. Some branches were clearly much bigger than this. At least 45

[43] RA, 374, 395. Technically a caporione is a head of one of the quarters of Rome.
[44] No references will be given for wills preserved in the ASV and entered in its card-index.
[45] BMV, MS Gradenigo Dolfin 134, 138.

members of the elite had 4 sons or more surviving infancy (girls tended to be under-reported in genealogies), and at least 60 proctors had 4 or more brothers each. But even the average branch was clearly bigger than the average Venetian household, which had only 3.7 members in the 1580s, and 4.5 members in 1642.[46]

Wills make many references to the 'honour of the house' (*l'honorevolezza della casa*). These words were not empty ones. The house was able to make considerable demands on the individual. A dramatic example is that of patriarch Zuan Dolfin, who began his career in the church but had to leave it because of the 'interests of his family'. According to a contemporary biography, he was needed to look after his younger brothers when his father was employed outside Venice.[47] Girls might be put into nunneries to save on their dowries, and men might not be able to marry because celibacy was the most reliable means of legitimate birth control. Thirty per cent of the elite never married, and the figure for the nobility as a whole in the same period is about 60 per cent.[48]

Like noble families elsewhere, Venetian noble families faced a dilemma. On one hand, too many children living in the style to which the family was accustomed risked the impoverishment of the house. Hence the growing use of *fedecommessi* (entails) which effectively established primogeniture at one remove; younger sons were provided for but their children were not. The effect was to discourage younger sons from marrying, and this risked the extinction of the house for lack of male heirs. It was difficult to find a strategy which avoided the two dangers of impoverishment and extinction.

The Venetian nobility as a whole seems to have preferred the second danger, and declined from 1,967 males over twenty-five in 1594 to 1,703 (in spite of the aggregations) in 1719. The elite, who tended to be richer than the average noble, married more frequently, but a number of the leading figures in this period were bachelors. Nicolò Contarini,* Lunardo Donà,* Francesco Erizzo,* Francesco da Molin,* Francesco Morosini,* Nicolò

---

[46]   Beltrami (1954), 188ff.
[47]   Gualdo Priorato (1659), s.v. 'Giovanni Delfino'.
[48]   Rodenwalt (1957).

Sagredo* are all examples. The cases of Erizzo,* da Molin* and Morosini* are a reminder of the obvious career for a noble bachelor outside the church – the navy.

The Venetian 'house' may be described as a 'collateral' type of family organization. The relationships which were stressed were brother–brother and uncle–nephew. There is plenty of evidence of this within the elite. Pasquale Cicogna* was very close to his brother Antonio. Lunardo Donà* was close to his brother Nicolò, who moved into the Doge's Palace when Lunardo was elected. Zuan Bembo,* another bachelor doge, was close to his brother Filippo, with whom he was buried and to whose sons he left his property. Nicolò Donà* was close to his brother Francesco and to Francesco's sons. The division of labour between brothers was a way in which the house could further the political career of one of its members (financial assistance was another). Battista Nani* was able to devote his energies to politics because his brother Agostino took over the running of the household, and Nicolò Contarini* was in a similar situation. The Senate recognized this 'special relationship' between brothers when it knighted Girolamo Corner* for the services of his dead brother Cattarino. The traditional form of trade organization in Venice, the *fraterna*, institutionalized the same relationship. No doubt this bond between brothers contributed to the development of huge kin groups or 'clans' like the Contarini.

There is much less to say about the family in Amsterdam, but this is significant in itself.[49] Trading companies were composed of individuals, not of families. Brothers traded for themselves. The four sons of Gerrit Bicker* all went into trade, but they divided the world between them and each kept to his area. Grown-up sons often lived in separate homes. The brothers Andries and Cornelis de Graeff* lived in the same street, the Herengracht, but in different houses, and they had different country houses too. Entails were known to the Amsterdam elite, but they seem to have been less important than in Venice – another sign of 'individualism'. A dead man's property would simply be divided among his children.

[49]   On the Dutch family, Woude (1972), Haks (1983).

Tax assessments in Amsterdam read very differently from those in Venice. In Venice a nobleman declares that he lives with his brothers in the family palace and then declares the family property, adding his 'speciality' or individual property if there is any. In Amsterdam individual brothers and even sisters would be assessed separately. Thus in the *kohier* of 1674 six members of the de Geer family, a man and five women, are assessed at 217 florins each. They had their financial independence. Property and housing are not everything, but at least they are valuable clues to a family structure. The general impression is one of individualism, in the sense of sons being independent of their fathers during their lifetime, and of younger sons being independent of their elder brothers.

Even daughters might show an independence unusual elsewhere. To take an example from nearby Delft, where the affair became a *cause célèbre*, burgomaster Geraldo Welhoek had to make great efforts to prevent his daughter from marrying the man of her choice against his will, and the couple did marry after his death.[50] The tax records suggest that the rich widow who was head of a household was an important Amsterdam phenomenon. In other words one may say that in Amsterdam the nuclear or 'conjugal' family was dominant – man, wife and unmarried children. There was relatively little contact with relatives, and the children had a more or less free choice of partners.[51] In Venice the dominant form of social organization was the extended family, covering several generations and including the married male children. In Venice the 'joint family' was dominant: residence was joint, so was consumption, and so was ownership. There was much more stress on the family in Venice than in Amsterdam. Families went back much further, whereas in Amsterdam it was difficult to take genealogies back earlier than the fifteenth century. Amsterdam was, after all, a fairly new city, its elite were not noble and were only just taking to the use of surnames in the sixteenth century.

The Venetian social system seems to have been oriented more towards the family, the Amsterdam system towards achievement. In Venice it was possible for men from certain families to become

---

[50]   Renier (1944), 161–79.
[51]   Haks (1983).

doge without really trying. Alvise Contarini,* Carlo Contarini* and Domenico Contarini* are all examples. No one at Amsterdam, not even the Bickers, had greatness thrust upon them in quite this way. In short, the distribution of wealth, status and power was made on different criteria in Venice and Amsterdam. The Venetian elite was part of a legally privileged estate of noblemen with considerable loyalty to their extended families. The Amsterdam elite was an informally defined governing group, part of a class rather than part of an estate, more individualistic and more achievement oriented, attaching less importance to family loyalties (particularly in the first half of the period) and defining 'family' in a much narrower way.

3

Political Functions

In Venice the elite ruled not just a city but an empire by sea and land. Crete and the Morea were the remains of the maritime empire (Cyprus had been lost in 1570, just before the period began). The empire on the mainland, or *terraferma,* included between 1.5 and 2 million people, some living in sizeable towns. Brescia had about 40,000 inhabitants in the mid seventeenth century, Padua about 30,000, Vicenza about 25,000.[1] Venice, in other words, was not so much a city as a territorial state, and the running of this state involved the elite in a variety of functions. It may be useful to distinguish four main functions – central government, local government, war and diplomacy – and to look at the offices held by members of the elite, or at least at the more important ones.

A hundred and fifty-one of the elite held important office in the central government as members of the College, the Senate or the Council of Ten. The College was a group of twenty-six men: the doge, his six councillors, the sixteen *savi* and the three heads of the *quarantia*. Five of the *savi* were particularly concerned with the mainland, and five were young men learning the art of government. The heads of the *quarantia* were judges. The Senate was concerned in particular with decisions about war and foreign policy, and the Council of Ten was concerned with crime.

---

[1] Beltrami (1954), 63ff.

A hundred and eleven of the elite held important office in local government, the government of the empire. Subject cities were allowed to retain their own laws and even their own town councils, but nobles from Venice were sent to administer them. Important cities had two *rettori* ('rulers'), a *podestà*, concerned with civil matters, and a *capitano*, concerned with military ones. The most honourable of these posts was *podestà* of Padua. One might compare the Venetian *rettori* with the French *intendants* of the seventeenth century, especially since their reports on the state of the region they governed were not the least important part of their jobs. The *provveditori generali* of Palma and Candia were more or less viceroys, governing Friuli and Crete respectively, and so they are included here rather than with the military appointments.

Seventy-five of the elite held important military or naval office. The Venetian elite was not composed entirely of 'foxes'. Famous examples of 'lions' are Zuan Bembo,* Francesco Erizzo,* Francesco da Molin* and, most celebrated of all, Francesco Morosini.* All four were elected doge after distinguished military careers, holding such offices as *capitano in golfo*, commanding naval forces in the Adriatic; *generale contra Uscocchi*, appointed to root out the Uskoks, Christian refugees from the Ottoman Empire turned pirates, operating from Senj and elsewhere on the coast of Dalmatia; *provveditore d'armata*, in command of a fleet; and *capitano generale da mar*, the naval commander-in-chief, appointed only in time of war (*provveditore generale da mar* was the highest peacetime appointment). The navy was a normal career for a Venetian nobleman and two posts on each galley were reserved for adolescent nobles. However, they did not monopolize officer posts; for example the Dane Curt Siversen was *tenente generale* in 1660.[2]

The land forces were not officered by Venetians. At the top one would usually find great nobles from other parts of Italy, such as Luigi d'Este, an infantry commander in 1614, or Alessandro Farnese, prince of Parma, who commanded the Venetian cavalry in the mid seventeenth century. One might find a foreign noble-man, like John Ernest of Nassau, commander of Dutch mercen-

[2] M. Nani Mocenigo (1935).

aries in 1617. Below them, the officers were mainly nobles from the mainland. Venetian nobles were attached to the army to supervise the professional commanders, as 'field commissioner' (*commissario in campo*), without whose consent the commander could not act, or, at the highest level, through an office which Francesco Erizzo held four times, *provveditore generale dell'esercito in terraferma*.[3]

Seventy-four of the elite were ambassadors at one time or another. Of the four fields, this is the one which seems most obviously dominated by the elite. Diplomats had a good chance of becoming proctors, and proctors had a good chance of being appointed diplomats. This is what one might have expected, since diplomats in seventeenth-century Europe had to be men of high status and considerable wealth.

There were offices which involved the administration of the city, held by members of the elite, but they were relatively unimportant. The *provveditori di notte*, for example, dealt with security in Venice. The proctors themselves had civic functions, such as almsgiving, and looking after the Church of San Marco, the Piazza and the Doge's Palace, but these duties were no longer an important part of their job. The city had been transformed by becoming the centre of a territorial state.

Finally, it is worth remarking that about 25 per cent of the elite held no important office at all, among them the wealthy music-loving Marco Contarini.* It is unlikely that he wanted to hold office. Since he was both rich and a Contarini, he could surely have held office had he wanted, so I presume he preferred to devote himself to music.

A point which needs emphasis is the number of times certain members of the elite held important office. Girolamo Zustinian,* for instance, was *savio del consiglio* thirteen times. If a man was appointed an ambassador once, he was likely to be appointed several times. Anzolo Contarini,* for example, was twice ambassador to Rome, twice to England, once to France and once to Emperor Ferdinand III. Members of the elite might hold two or three offices at once. Agostino Nani* was appointed proctor in 1612. In the five years from 1612 to 1616 he held office fifteen

---

[3] Mallett and Hale (1984).

times. Thus in 1612 he was a *savio*, an ambassador extraordinary and 'reformer of studies' of the University of Padua.[4]

This spread of offices in a single year is a reminder that in Venice the four main political sectors – central government, local government, war and diplomacy – were not exclusive of one another. Like the traditional Chinese mandarin or the English civil servant, the Venetian patrician was an all-rounder rather than a specialist, an amateur rather than a professional. Nine of the elite held important office in all four sectors and forty-seven held office in three of them. There was a place in the political system for the specialist in naval affairs, like Francesco Morosini,* and a place for the financial expert, like Zuanfrancesco Priuli,* governor of the Mint, who was elected proctor because he found a way to redeem the public debt.

More distinctively Venetian, however, are the all-rounders, including doges Lunardo Donà,* Francesco Erizzo,* Antonio Priuli* and Bertucci Valier.* Donà, for instance, was ambassador to Spain, *capitano* of Brescia, *savio* and *provveditore generale di terraferma*. Antonio Priuli* commanded a galley, joined the Council of Ten, was sent as ambassador to France and was appointed *capitano* of Padua. Two distinguished diplomats, Battista Nani* and Simone Contarini,* were asked to be *capitano generale da mar*, the supreme naval appointment, without having had naval experience. Both refused, but what is significant is that they should have been asked at all. Nicolò Contarini* held his first military appointment at the age of sixty-four, in the war against the Habsburgs in 1617.[5]

To use the language of 'political functions' risks giving a false impression. The elite were not completely disinterested servants of the public. Many of them wanted power and as a group they exercised power at the expense of other people. A zero-sum conception of power is as necessary to the historian or political scientist as a functional conception. Excluded from power were three groups: the lower nobility, the commoners of Venice and the subject population, noble and commoner, of the Venetian empire.[6]

---

[4] F. Nani Mocenigo (1894), 100.
[5] Cozzi (1958), 149ff.
[6] Contrast Davis (1962), ch. 1, with Pullan (1964).

The lesser nobility were not, in theory, excluded from power at all. The traditional view of the Venetian constitution (of which the most famous expression is the sixteenth-century treatise by Gasparo Contarini) was that it was a mixed constitution, in which the doge represented the monarchical element, the Senate the aristocratic element and the Greater Council the democratic element. In the early seventeenth century the political writer Traiano Boccalini also emphasized that Venice was a meritocracy in the sense that any noble could aspire to high office.[7] Not everyone accepted this view, though it may have functioned as an ideology helping to maintain the elite in power. Jean Bodin, with his gift for penetrating below the surface of political reality, argued in the later sixteenth century that Venice had been in turn monarchy and democracy but that it had 'changed into an aristocracy, and that in such quiet sort, that it was not well by any man perceived that the estate was at all changed'.[8] Similarly, an anonymous treatise on the government of Venice, written about 1660, declares that Venice is an oligarchy which conceals the fact (oligarchia . . . in modo . . . segreto e latente).[9]

To decide this question in a satisfactory manner it would be necessary to make a statistical study of elections to a wide range of offices over a long period, a study better undertaken by a group than by an individual historian. The more provisional conclusions of the last chapter were that it was not impossible for an able nobleman who was not from a rich or powerful branch of his family to enter the elite, but that it was much easier for the wealthy and the well connected, that the contemporary distinction between an upper nobility (the grandi) and the rest had substance. The lesser nobles resented their exclusion from power and on occasion worked together against the grandi. The constitutional conflict of 1582, for instance, when the Council of Ten and its 'junta' lost power over foreign policy and finance to the Senate, was to some degree a conflict between greater and lesser nobility; the continuance of the junta was supported by 'the greater senators with their clients and relations'.[10]

[7]   G. Contarini (1543); Boccalini (1910–48), bk 1, chs 5, 25; bk 2, ch. 39.
[8]   Bodin (1576), bk 4, ch. 1.
[9]   Bacco (1856).
[10]   Molin, 119, but cf. Lowry (1972).

In the late sixteenth century the Venetian nobility came close to splitting into two groups, though these groups were not formally organized like political parties. Several different conflicts came near to fusion at this time. There was the clash between an older generation, the *vecchi*, versus a younger one, the *giovani*. There was the structural conflict between the greater nobles and the lesser. There were also what might be called the 'conjunctural' conflicts of the time, supporters of Spain versus supporters of France and the devout versus the anti-clerical.[11]

Another instance of 'the lack of harmony that is seen nowadays between the greater and the lesser nobles' (*i grandi e la nobiltà minore*) was the conflict between the Senate and the Greater Council in 1656. The Senate appointed Antonio Bernardo* to be *capitano generale da mar*, but the Greater Council chose Lazzaro Mocenigo instead.[12] Yet another possible example is that of the failure of Zuan Sagredo* to become doge twenty years later, despite having mobilized a formidable group of relatives in support of his attempt. Twenty-eight out of forty-one voters supported him in the election, in 1676, and Sagredo* had already begun to receive the congratulations of well-wishers when a popular demonstration against his election took place (whether spontaneous or organized by his enemies). The Greater Council decided to hold the election again, and Alvise Contarini* was elected instead. The problem is to decide who Sagredo's* opponents were – the people, the lesser nobles or rival grandees.[13]

The most famous example of the lesser nobles as a force in politics in this period, however, is to be found in the early seventeenth century, in the movement associated with Renier Zen.* In 1625 the wealthy and pious Zuan Corner* was elected doge. He favoured his relations more than was customary for doges to do, and he was attacked by Zen,* who went on to describe the enormous gulf between the greater and lesser nobles.[14] Zen* had the ear of the Greater Council; on one occasion he rose, spoke for four hours and was heard with 'marvellous attention'; a contemporary estimated that nearly two-thirds of the Greater Council

---

11   Cozzi (1958), 4–18; Bouwsma (1968), 268ff.
12   Bacco (1856), 35.
13   Romanin (1853–61), vol. 7, 477–80; Mattozzi (1977).
14   Cozzi (1958); Rose (1974).

belonged to his 'faction'.[15] It was said that he wanted to depose the Doge, and the danger was taken seriously enough for one of the Doge's sons to try to assassinate him in 1627. The faction of the poor nobles declared that they were unable to enter the Council of Ten, and demanded entry.

Despite these dramatic statements and threats, all that happened was a minor change to the position of the Council of Ten; Zen's* election as proctor (1628); and, when Zuan Corner* died in 1629, his succession by Nicolò Contarini,* who was not one of the *grandi* and who was elected with the help of the votes of the supporters of Zen,* another candidate in this election. All the same, the Zen* movement tells us a good deal about the structure of Venetian politics, as open conflicts often do.[16]

In the first place, it is worth noting that the leader of the poor nobles was not one of them. Renier Zen* was not elected a proctor till his movement was well under way, but he was well connected, allied to important branches of the Barbarigo and Contarini clans, and he had already served as an ambassador in Savoy and Rome before 1625. In the second place, the conflict shows how the lesser nobles were able to put pressure on the greater. In the third place, however, it reveals how weak this pressure was. It is natural to wonder why the movement of the lesser nobles fizzled out so easily. One possible explanation is in the strength of cross-cutting social ties. The 'horizontal solidarity' of poor nobles and rich nobles was balanced by the 'vertical solidarity' of patrons and clients. Zen* had his clients, but Corner* had his. A lesser noble would be torn between allegiance to his social group and allegiance to his patron. As a distinguished social anthropologist has remarked, conflicting allegiances are often a force making for social cohesion, because a man caught in such a conflict has a strong interest in seeing that any given dispute is settled by a compromise.[17] Cross-linking of this kind may well be the fundamental reason for the relative absence of political conflict in Venice. It is also a reminder not to exaggerate the cohesiveness of the elite.

[15] Venier, 119; Cozzi (1958), 247n.
[16] Cozzi (1958), ch. 6.
[17] Gluckman (1956), ch. 1.

There is less to say about the ways in which the elite was able to exclude from power the commoners of Venice and the subject population of the mainland. 'Divide and rule' seems to have been their fundamental maxim. The commoners of Venice can be divided into the citizens and the rest. The citizens were some 5 per cent of the population of Venice, in other words scarcely more numerous than the nobles. They were excluded from the Greater Council, but their ambitions were satisfied in a number of ways. For example, as one late-sixteenth-century political writer, Giovanni Botero, suggested, the religious fraternities, or *scuole*, helped satisfy the citizens by drawing them and the nobles together.[18] Certain offices were reserved for citizens, including that of the grand chancellor, and the posts of secretary to the Council of Ten, to the Senate and to ambassadors. This last post was a responsible one, since if an ambassador died *en poste*, his secretary might take over.

These offices (apart from secretaries to ambassadors) were for life. Given the rapid rotation of office among the nobles, the secretaries were in a position rather like senior civil servants as compared with ministers in Britain today. Some of them appear to have enjoyed considerable power. It was said that the secretaries of the Council of Ten supported the continuance of the junta in 1582 because their power was threatened by the reform movement.[19] Renier Zen* denounced the rule of the secretaries, perhaps thinking in particular of Zuanbattista Padavino, secretary to the Council of Ten from 1584 onwards, whom he thought responsible for a sentence of banishment passed on him.[20] One of the few new families to enter not only the nobility but also the elite in this period, the Ottobon, was a family of citizens who had served as chancellors or secretaries.

Robbed of their natural leaders the citizens, the people (that 'many-headed monster', as the elite viewed it) was less dangerous.[21] Gasparo Contarini explained the absence of conflict between nobles and common people in Venice by impartial justice and a regular corn supply. Doges and proctors threw money to the

---

[18] Botero (1595), fos 41, 97, 107–8; cf. Pullan (1964), 103, (1971), 626.
[19] Molin, 119ff.
[20] Cozzi (1958), 265ff.
[21] Relatione 2, fo. 139r.

people when they were elected. The old custom of the election of
a fishermen's doge, who was solemnly received and kissed by the
real doge, might be seen as a device for persuading the people they
participated in a system from which they were in reality excluded.
One seventeenth-century writer was cynical enough to suggest that
the government encouraged the two factions of the common people, the Castellani (from Castello, the sailors' quarter) and the
Nicolotti (from San Nicolò, the fishermen's parish), with their
annual fist-fights, in order to keep the people divided.[22]

Similar devices were used to control the nobles and the common
people of the mainland, with varying degrees of success. As Botero
pointed out, the privileges of the cities of the mainland were not
abolished under Venetian rule.[23] Local noblemen could still become town councillors. The Venetian *rettori* deliberately frater-
nized with the local nobles. Some of them were admitted to the
Venetian nobility. The Savorgnan, a powerful family from Friuli,
had already entered before our period began, and the 'aggregations' of the later seventeenth century included the Angarani
(nobles from Vicenza), the Bressa (nobles from Treviso), the
Ghirardini (nobles from Verona) and many others.[24] Again, nobles
from the mainland could and often did make a career in the armed
forces of the Republic.

In practice, local nobles often continued to exercise considerable power. The *rettori* held office for too short a time to get to
know their areas, let alone control them. To take just one example: Count Francesco Martinengo Colleoni was a power to be
reckoned with near his castle of Cavernago, in the Bergamo area,
early in the seventeenth century. He had men killed with impunity.
The Council of Ten issued instructions for his arrest in 1619, but
the *rettori* did not carry out this order, writing to excuse themselves: 'Cavernago is a strong place with moat and draw-bridge so
that hundreds of men would be needed to surround it . . . There is
armour for a hundred and a number of arquebuses.'[25]

On the mainland, as in the city, the Venetian government seems
to have adopted a policy of 'divide and rule'. When Francesco

22 Relatione 1, fo. 77v.
23 Botero (1595), fos 43ff.
24 ASV, Misc. Cod. III and Cod. Soranzo 15.
25 Belotti (1940), 54.

Erizzo* was administering Friuli, he is said to have advised the government to create some nobles counts but to exclude others in order to create bad feeling and so prevent the local elite from presenting a united front.[26] A seventeenth-century *Opinion*, once attributed to Fra Paolo Sarpi, warns the Venetian government against Padua, Verona and Treviso and suggests that 'it is convenient to make show of administering justice impartially to them, but never to let slip any occasion of humbling them', and that, if the leaders of the discontented can be identified, 'let all occasions be laid hold on for exterminating them . . . it will be more prudent to employ poison instead of a hangman, because the advantage will be the same and the hatred the less'.[27]

Whether the Venetian government regularly employed poison as a means of control may be doubted, and this text is more likely to be a satire than a detached description. Discontented nobles there certainly were, however. For example, a certain Paulo Zagallo at Campolongo in 1646 declared that the Venetians were 'long-nosed busybodies' (*becconazzi fatudi*) and that he would prefer to live under Spanish rule. One wonders how many people thought like him but were too cautious to say so; he was banished for his outburst.[28] On the other hand, clashes between the common people and the nobility of the mainland, as at Brescia in 1644, worked to the advantage of the Venetians.[29] Once more we see that cross-cutting conflicts led to relative stability.

In Amsterdam, by contrast, the political functions of the elite, especially their official functions, were narrower in range. They were city oriented, as a list of the main offices makes abundantly clear. Besides the burgomasters and councillors, there was one *schout* (sheriff) and nine *schepenen* (magistrates). There were also treasurers, ordinary and extraordinary; masters of the orphans (*weesmeesteren*); masters of insurance (*assurantiemeesteren*); and commissioners for marital affairs (*huwelijksche zaken*), maritime affairs (*zeezaken*), the exchange bank (*wisselbank*), the lending bank (*bank van leening*), the excise (*accijns*) and bankruptcy

---

[26] Relatione 1, fo. 84v.
[27] Sarpi (1788), Eng. trans., London (1707), 55.
[28] Borgherini-Scarabellin (1917), 42.
[29] Ventura (1964), 385, 469ff.

(*desolate boedels*). At the end of the period the office of postmaster became a desirable one.

To be a commissioner was for many a step on the ladder leading to the Council and even the burgomastership. Nearly 20 per cent of the elite administered almshouses at some point in their career, before or after becoming councillors: the Leprozenhuis, for example, the house for lepers; or the Sint Joris Hof. Others were in charge of the houses of punishment for men and women, the Rasphuis and the Spinhuis respectively.

At first sight the military functions of the Amsterdam elite appear much more important than in Venice. Nearly two-thirds of the group were officers in the civic guard (the *burgerij* or *schutterij*), usually as ensigns or lieutenants before becoming councillors, and in higher ranks after they had joined the elite. However, we should not take membership of the civic guard (perhaps 'trained bands' would be a better translation) too seriously. Indeed, thanks to painters like Rembrandt and Van de Helst it is impossible to forget that the civic guard, in Amsterdam and elsewhere, was more of a club than a military institution, and that its officers were more able to brandish a fork or a wineglass than a sword or a halberd. On one of the rare occasions that they were really needed, the French invasion of 1672, the Dutch *schutterij* were not particularly effective.[30] The institution looks like a good example of the play element in culture, so well analysed by Huizinga, though he does not cite this particular instance.[31] This impression is confirmed when we find that two sons of burgomasters were appointed captains of infantry in the Amsterdam garrison at the ages of five and nine respectively. Such offices were a way of rewarding clients as well as relatives. A contemporary attack on the Bickers accuses them of inserting their men as officers of the civic guard.[32]

On the other hand, these military activities should not be dismissed altogether. It is easy to scoff at merchants dressed up as soldiers, and at a civic guard which did not defend anything. To be fair, we should be aware that some of the paintings of a carousing

---

[30]   Roorda (1961), 70ff.
[31]   Huizinga (1938).
[32]   J. E. Elias (1923), 202; K.6773, 4.

militia were representations of a major occasion for rejoicing, the official end of the war with Spain in 1648. We also need to remember the importance of the *schutterij* in the coup of 1578, when the new men and the religious exiles took over the government of Amsterdam. Nor should we forget that some members of the elite knew about warfare. Before they entered city politics, J. E. Huydecoper* was an ensign of foot and Ferdinand van Collen* a cornet of dragoons. After his bankruptcy Diederick Tholincx* left Amsterdam and joined the army. Dirck Bas,* Ferdinand van Collen* and Nicolaes Witsen* were 'field deputies' (civilian supervisors of military operations not unlike the Venetian *commissario in campo*). The sons of Pieter Hasselaer,* Dirck de Vlaming* and Cornelis van Vlooswijck* all took up military careers. There were also naval officers in the elite, such as Jacob van Neck,* Laurens Reael* and Wijbrand Warwijck.*

The political functions of the Amsterdam elite do not look very grand compared to the Venetian. However, the contrast was not as great in practice as it was formally. Indeed, as it was argued above (p. 7), the Italian model of a city dominating the *contado*, the countryside round about it, is a useful one for understanding the position of Amsterdam in the seventeenth century.

At the most precise – if least important – level, it is worth drawing attention to the fact that the Amsterdam elite exercised certain rights over pieces of nearby countryside. The burgomasters were permanent feoffees (*erfleenheeren*) of certain manors (*ambachtsheerlijkheden*). Amstelveen is a well-known example, and Gerard Schaep* certainly thought that Amsterdam's rights over Amstelveen were not to be despised.[33] In a similar way, the office of bailiff (*drost*) of the nearby castle of Muiden was in the gift of the burgomasters, and C. P. Hooft* obtained it for his son, the poet and historian who made the 'Muiden circle' (*Muiderkring*) of such importance in Dutch cultural history. Again, F. H. Oetgens* had his son made *poldermeester*, the official in charge of the polders near Amsterdam.

All the same, to call Amsterdam a 'city-state' is to say something both more important and more vague. The resolutions of the Council show that the councillors did not spend all their time

[33] Schaep (1655), 356ff.

talking about almshouses. At the beginning of the eighteenth century they spend a good deal of time talking about the Spanish Succession and the value of a defensive alliance between the Dutch Republic, Britain and Sweden.[34] Why? Because, to oversimplify for the sake of clarity, the councillors ruled Amsterdam, Amsterdam ruled Holland and Holland ruled the United Provinces. In theory, the Dutch Republic was a federation in which the seven provinces were equal, and in theory Amsterdam was only one of eighteen towns in the province of Holland.[35] In practice, however, the Amsterdam elite had ways of getting what they wanted. After all, Amsterdam paid about 44 per cent of the taxes of the province of Holland, and the province of Holland (from 1612, when the quota was fixed) paid 57 per cent of the taxes of the whole Dutch Republic. In other words, one city paid 25 per cent of the taxes of the whole nation.

Amsterdam sent representatives to certain institutions of the province of Holland. In the first place, to the States of Holland. There were nineteen deputations to the States, one from the nobility of the province (the *Ridderschap*) and one each from eighteen towns. A town deputation usually consisted of a burgomaster or ex-burgomaster, the town pensionary (or legal adviser) and some other members of the Town Council. However many people made up the deputation, the town had one vote. Four towns were usually independent of Amsterdam in their policies – Dordrecht, Haarlem, Delft and Leiden. On the other hand, the lead of Amsterdam was usually followed by the thirteen smaller towns, such as Alkmaar, Hoorn, Gouda or Schiedam, and thus the policy of Amsterdam became the policy of the States of Holland.

This point about the predominance of Amsterdam is often made, but it may be useful to approach the problem in a more oblique and unusual way, through the collective biography of the elite. For example, fifty members of the elite held office in the Council in Committee (*Gecommiteerde Raaden*) of the province of Holland, which dealt with taxation and defence. It was divided into two colleges, for the north and south of the province. Of the

[34] GA, Vroedschap, Resolutiën, vols for 1700–1702.
[35] Fockema Andreae (1961).

ten members of the college of the Southern Region (*Zuider-Kwartier*), one was always from Amsterdam. Other important offices in the province were also filled by members of the elite. Thus Gerrit Delft* was treasurer-general of Holland in 1580. Fifty-one members of the elite held office in a local admiralty, usually Amsterdam or Zeeland.

The province of Holland in turn sent representatives to certain federal institutions, of which the most important were the States-General (in which the seven provinces had equal representation) and the Council of State (*Raad van State*), which had twelve members, of whom three were from Holland. To the States-General went fifteen burgomasters and councillors such as Willem Baerdesen,* Reynier Cant,* Andries Bicker,* Nicolaes Witsen* and Jacob Valckenier.* To the Council of State went fourteen of the elite – including Jacob van Neck,* Reynier Cant,* Vincent van Bronckhorst,* Hendrick Hudde* and Jacob Hinlopen.*[36] Attendance at the Council of State was a particularly demanding duty, and Bronckhorst* and Hudde* both resigned from the Town Council when they were appointed; they had to spend too much time in The Hague. Similarly, Coenraed Burgh* resigned to take up the important federal appointment of treasurer-general of the Union.

It has more than once been suggested that appointment to these posts outside the city was a kind of banishment for leaders of a losing faction in the Town Council. As C. P. Hooft* put it, 'To the college of the Council in Committee in The Hague . . . were sent ex-burgomasters that people seemed to want to do without here' (*dye men schijnt hyer liefst te willen missen*).[37] The argument from chronology supports this suggestion. Gerrit Witsen* was sent off to the Council in 1617, after criticizing the policies of the powerful F. H. Oetgens.* Cornelis Bicker* was sent in 1651, just after the Prince of Orange had had him removed from the Town Council. Henrick Hooft* was sent when the opposing Valckenier faction was in power, and when Hooft* came to the top again in 1672, it was the turn of Gillis Valckenier* to be sent to the Council in Committee.

---

[36] On Van Neck's activities in the Council, Terpstra (1960), 138ff, 165ff.
[37] C. P. Hooft (1871–1925), vol. 1, 70.

However, it may still be argued that membership of these provincial and federal bodies helped the elite to influence, if not to dominate, the rest of the Republic, in matters of foreign policy in particular. Members of the elite sometimes played a crucial political role in Dutch affairs; indeed, the Union of Utrecht, from which the United Provinces derived, was negotiated in part by one of them, Reynier Cant,* councillor first to William the Silent and then to Maurice of Nassau. Again, it was in the crucial years from 1646 onwards, when peace negotiations were in progress, that the powerful Andries Bicker* headed the Holland deputation to the States-General.

Their role as diplomats was another means by which members of the elite were able to influence the affairs of the whole United Provinces, so that the trading interests of the Amsterdammers were reflected in the foreign policy of the Republic. Twenty-four members of the elite served as diplomats in the period. At the time of the war between Denmark and Sweden in 1644, for example, the ambassadors to these two powers were Andries Bicker* and Gerard Schaep.* Albert Burgh* was ambassador to Russia and to Denmark. Joan Huydecoper,* hampered by his ignorance of German, was ambassador to Brandenburg, and so on.

Another means whereby Amsterdam and its elite were able to influence the rest of the Republic was via the East and West India Companies and the Society of Surinam.[38] Like the Republic itself, these companies had a federal structure. There were regional 'chambers', each with their directors, from whom were chosen the directors of the company as a whole, the XVII of the East India Company (Vereenigde Oost-Indische Compagnie, or VOC), and the XIX of the West India Company (West-Indische Compagnie, or WIC). Amsterdam never had an absolute majority of the XVII, and the meetings of the VOC were held at Middelburg as well as at Amsterdam. In practice, once again, the power of Amsterdam was greater than it was on paper. The Amsterdam chambers of the VOC and the WIC were by far the most important. Amsterdam put up 57 per cent of the capital of the VOC at its foundation. In any case, eight of the XVII always came from Amsterdam.

---

[38]   Dillen (1958); Hoboken (1960); Dillen (1961); R. van Gelder (1993).

Amsterdammers also infiltrated into the other chambers, whether as an insurance policy to protect their investments or as a means to gain control. For instance, in the late seventeenth century Amsterdammers owned about 38 per cent of the capital of the Zeeland chamber of the VOC. In 1719 A. Velters* had 74,000 florins invested in the Delft chamber of the VOC. At any rate, 103 of the elite, about 30 per cent, were directors of the VOC or the WIC or the Society of Surinam. This meant Amsterdam had influence on the government of an empire much more extensive than that of Venice. Of eighteen governors-general of the Netherlands Indies from 1609 to 1718, three came from Amsterdam regent families. Laurens Reael,* son of a councillor, ruled the East Indies from 1616 onwards and later entered the Town Council himself. Coenraed Burgh* left it to become governor of Curaçao.[39]

In 1650 a pamphlet expressed the fear that 'the great fish Amsterdam might eat up the smaller ones', and that the rulers of Amsterdam (the Bickers in particular) had designs to make themselves the rulers of the state, and create another Venice. Hysterical in tone, exaggerated in its claims, this pamphlet expressed a fear of the elite which had some basis in reality.[40] But how much? To answer this question we need to follow the advice of Robert Dahl (above, pp. 3–4), and to identify situations where there was a conflict between Amsterdam and the rest of the Republic.

For example, in the 1590s leading Amsterdammers were engaged in trade with Spain, despite the fact that the Republic was at war with Spain at the time. The ships taking corn to Spain simply sailed under false flags. In 1596 there was a conflict between the States-General, which forbade the export of corn to Spain and Italy, and the rulers of Amsterdam, who objected; it was Amsterdam which won.[41] A few years later the decision went the other way. Although the Town Council of Amsterdam had declared on 22 March 1607 that peace meant 'the irreparable damage and decline of these lands', they could not prevent the Twelve Years' Truce with Spain, which lasted from 1609 to 1621. In the late

[39] Rhede (1891).
[40] K.6773, 5–6.
[41] J. H. Kernkamp (1931–4), vol. 2, 190ff.

1620s, when the question of war or peace with Spain was again on the agenda, Amsterdam once more failed to get its way, but in this case it is only fair to add that the Town Council was itself divided on this issue. In 1627, when the Admiralty proposed the standardization of naval construction, Amsterdam successfully resisted it.[42] In 1644, the Amsterdam elite were able to involve the Dutch Republic in the war between Sweden and Denmark when the Dutch ambassadors to the two belligerents were burgomasters of Amsterdam. Their aim was to force the King of Denmark to lower the tolls he levied on Dutch ships passing through the Sound.[43]

In other cases, as so often in politics, conflicts were complicated by the fact that more than two groups were involved, as will be seen by taking a few famous examples in chronological order. In 1619 Jan van Oldenbarnevelt, grand pensionary of Holland, was tried and executed for treason. This was the climax of the conflict between Oldenbarnevelt and the Stadholder, Maurice of Nassau, a clash of a peace policy with a war policy, and of a relatively tolerant form of Calvinism with an intolerant form. Some of the Amsterdam elite had come into conflict with Oldenbarnevelt, who supported Le Maire's Australian Company, a competitor with the VOC, and opposed the foundation of a West India Company when the question was discussed about 1607. One of Oldenbarnevelt's judges was Reynier Pauw,* a burgomaster of Amsterdam, a fiery Calvinist, a founder-member of the VOC who was interested in the West Indies trade as well. However, the Amsterdam Town Council were not unanimous in support of Maurice of Nassau. Indeed, he purged the Council in 1618, removing eight men and replacing them with his own appointments.[44]

Maurice's successor as stadholder, Prince Frederick Henry, once declared, 'I have no greater enemies than the town of Amsterdam.' He clashed in particular with burgomaster Andries Bicker.* The Prince wanted centralized control over the local admiralties, but Bicker* opposed him. The Prince wanted to forbid the sale of ships to Spain, but Bicker* and his colleagues Abraham Boom* and Jan Geelvinck* engaged in this trade. The Prince wanted to

[42] Méchoulan (1993), 114.
[43] Brugmans (1897–1905), 61.
[44] J. E. Elias (1923), 79ff.

continue the war with Spain, but Bicker* wanted to make peace, which is what finally happened in 1648. Following the peace, there was a clash between the rulers of Amsterdam and the new Stadholder, William II, because Amsterdam wanted to reduce the army and he did not. It was this conflict which led to the most spectacular confrontation in 1650, when William II sent an army against Amsterdam to depose the 'Bicker league'.[45]

In the period without a stadholder that followed William's death the most powerful man in the Republic, the Grand Pensionary, Jan de Witt, was allied to the Amsterdam elite through his marriage, in 1655, to Wendela Bicker, daughter of the former burgomaster Jan Bicker,* niece of Cornelis de Graeff* and sister-in-law of Jean Deutz.*[46] When William III became Stadholder in 1672, clashes with Amsterdam began again. In that year he removed ten men from the Town Council, including the Bicker ally Andries de Graeff,* replacing them with his nominees. In spite of this purge, clashes between Amsterdam and William continued in the 1680s, when Amsterdam supported a peace policy and opposed the levy of troops.[47]

These conflicts would be an excellent means of testing the power of the elite if only it had been cohesive. In fact it was split into parties, or – to use a term with fewer misleading modern overtones – into factions, in other words groups which are informally organized and relatively short-lived.[48] The Prince of Orange was able to purge the Council in 1618 because he had the support of the faction led by Reynier Pauw,* and his successor was able to carry out a similar coup in 1672 because he had the support of the faction led by Gillis Valckenier.*

Unfortunately, we do not know very much about these factions, and it is particularly hard to tell whether the conflict between factions was a conflict over policies or just a struggle for office. The problem is that differences of opinion between burgomasters or councillors were not recorded in the minutes of meetings.[49] In one case we do have good evidence of a conflict over policy, in

45   J. E. Elias, 112ff.
46   Rowen (1986).
47   J. E. Elias (1923), 173ff.
48   Nicholson (1969). Contrast Roorda (1961).
49   N. de Roever (1889).

precisely what Dahl regards as the key area of urban redevelopment. C. P. Hooft* attacked F. H. Oetgens* and his friends for the 'private profit' they made in real estate thanks to their inside knowledge, a knowledge they owed to their political position (below, p. 68). In other cases we know about religious conflicts within the Council (below, pp. 106–7).

However divided in other respects, the elite were united in their fear of 'the mob' (het grauw). An undated late-seventeenth-century report by the colonels of the civic guard deals with the measures to be taken in the event of rioting or plundering.[50] In 1617 the houses of some leading Amsterdammers, Arminian in religion, had been attacked and plundered, possibly with the encouragement of their religious opponents. Amsterdam was a port, and so liable to be the scene of sailors' riots, as it was, for example, in 1624, 1628, 1652 and 1696. After the de Witt brothers had been done to death by a crowd in The Hague in 1672, the Amsterdam elite must have slept less soundly at night. All the same, it was not part of their style to distract the many-headed monster with carnivals or by scattering money when burgomasters were elected, as Venetians did. For the preservation of public order, they simply relied on the civic guard.[51]

In both Amsterdam and Venice there were clashes between centre and periphery, metropolis and empire. However, comparison is complicated by the fact one cannot refer to Amsterdam as the 'centre' without qualification. It may have been what the Habsburg pamphleteer Lisola called it, the *primum mobile* of Holland, but The Hague was its rival as the centre of government of both the province and the federation. It was in The Hague that the States of Holland, the Council in Committee, the States-General and the Council of State all met. The Hague was also the seat of the stadholder's court. The doge was part of the Venetian elite, but his Dutch equivalent, the stadholder, was quite outside the Amsterdam elite and sometimes clashed violently with it.

It is clear that the governing elites of Venice and Amsterdam were not just town councillors. They dominated empires. The Venetians ruled the 1.5 to 2 million people living on the mainland.

---

[50] GA, J. Hudde, Brieven en papieren, no. 42.
[51] Dekker (1982).

For their part, the Amsterdammers dominated the 700,000 inhabitants of the province of Holland, if not the 2 million inhabitants of the whole United Provinces. This dominance was institutionalized in Venice through the *rettori* of the subject cities. In the case of Amsterdam, influence was less formal. Burgomasters might go on embassy and naval officers enter the Council, but the city did not control either diplomacy or the navy, as was the case in Venice. In other words, in its political as in its social structure, Venice was a more formal society, Amsterdam a more informal one.

4

Economic Base

In his famous study of the circulation of elites Vilfredo Pareto distinguished 'rentiers' from 'speculators' (or entrepreneurs). This distinction was partly made on the basis of attitude – rentiers were defined as unimaginative conservatives, entrepreneurs as imaginative innovators. It was also made in terms of two contrasted economic bases. Rentiers are men on fixed incomes; entrepreneurs are men whose incomes vary with the efforts they make to pursue profit. This may be a case of economic determinism, but it need not be. A variable income is likely to stimulate the imagination, but then a man who enjoys innovating is likely to prefer opportunities for profit to an income which is fixed. In this comparative case-study of elites it is obviously important to find out whether Venetians and Amsterdammers were predominantly rentiers or predominantly entrepreneurs. It would also be useful to know how wealthy the two groups were relative to one another and relative to other groups in the two communities.

To discover the wealth of the Venetian elite and the sources from which it was derived, there is no better evidence than their tax returns, despite warnings that they are 'too sporadic' and 'difficult to consult'.[1] Venetians paid the *decima*, a tenth of their annual income from 'immovable goods', essentially houses and land. The *decima* was assessed in 1581, 1661 and 1711 – in fact

---

[1] Davis (1962); cf. Canal (1908).

it should have been assessed much more often – and the returns made by each head of household still survive.[2] Although the inhabitants of the mainland paid a different tax, Venetians paid the *decima* on their property in the mainland too, so (cheating apart) a fairly complete picture of their land and houses – though not of their total income – should be given by this source. Even the head of state had to declare his income, a procedure surely unique in Europe.

In 1581 the doge and seventeen proctors returned their income; in 1711 the doge and thirty-seven proctors did so. They represent virtually the whole elite at the beginning and at the end of the period, hence I shall assume that they represent a fair sample of the whole. They were not an economic group in themselves, but most of them belonged to the group of large property owners.

The land, to take this first, tended to come in scattered pieces. This may have been deliberate policy, to insure against local disasters to crops. Venetians owned land most of all in the Padua and Treviso areas, near at hand, but they also owned substantial amounts near Vicenza and Verona, in the Polesine (towards Ferrara) and as far away as Friuli (towards Trieste). Estates tended to be broken into tiny fragments. Marco Contarini's* estate at Piazzola, for example, was divided into 111 parts. The estates were cultivated by the local peasants, usually for a fixed rent in kind but sometimes for a money rent or on a share-cropping basis, which made difficulties for the landowners compiling their tax returns; they had to calculate their average income over five years. Leases tended to be short, for five years or less, a procedure recommended in at least one of the agricultural treatises of the time.[3] The crops grown included wheat, rye, sorghum, millet, oil, wine and, towards the end of the period, maize, or *sorgo turco* as it was usually called. There are many references in the documents to chickens and pigs, often as *regalia*, or customary presents from tenant to landlord; but there are a few references to other livestock.

Urban property consisted of houses and shops in Venice, or

[2] Microfilms of these returns were deposited in the library of the University of Sussex in 1973.
[3] Agostinetti (1679), 58ff.

more rarely in other towns, such as Padua. It ranged from palaces let to fellow-nobles to tiny shops, like the hat shop on the bridge at the Rialto owned by Lunardo Donà.* On the whole it seems to have been less important than land.

As for the amount of income derived from these sources, the eighteen members of the elite who declared their income in 1581 averaged about 1,300 ducats a year each, from Marco Grimani* at 330 ducats to Gerolamo da Mula* at 3,300. The thirty-eight elite members of 1711 averaged 7,500 ducats a year each, from Piero Zen* at 1,257 ducats to Alvise Pisani* at 35,000. It is not easy to calculate the relative value of the ducat in 1581 and 1711. Italian prices rose steeply between 1580 and 1600, but they tended to fall after 1620 or 1630.[4] The most realistic way to assess these sums is perhaps to compare them with the annual earnings of a journeyman mason in Venice in the late sixteenth and early seventeenth centuries, about 50 and 70 ducats respectively.[5]

In fact the contrast was still greater, because the tax returns are not concerned with 'movable goods' (beni mobili). Movables included silver, jewels and money deposited in the Mint for safe-keeping (and 5 per cent interest) or invested in business or lent to private individuals, and declared or disguised as 'leases' (livelli).[6] A certain amount of information about movable goods can be gleaned from wills. A few examples will suggest the importance of the money deposited at the Mint. It is referred to in the wills of Zuan da Lezze* (died 1625); Antonio Grimani,* who made his will in 1624 and told his heirs to leave the money there; Alvise Barbarigo* (died 1678); Gerolamo Basadonna* (died 1697), whose wife's dowry, 12,000 ducats, was deposited there; Alvise da Mosto* (died 1701), who had deposited the vast sum of 39,000 ducats; and Ferigo Corner* (died 1708). Wills also refer to other forms of investment, such as the 'matured shares' (rate maturate) mentioned by Ferigo Corner* in 1708, which may have been something like a deferred annuity.[7] Unfortunately, wills, with their vague reference to the 'residue', rarely allow us to calculate the total wealth of the testator, so that there is no way of assessing

---

[4]   Romano (1968).
[5]   Pullan (1968), 158.
[6]   Pullan (1973).
[7]   I owe this suggestion to Brian Pullan.

the relative importance of movable and immovable goods in the wealth of the elite.

It is, once again, mainly from wills that the historian can glean a little information about the trading activities of patricians. At least a few proctors were involved in trade with the Middle East of the traditional Venetian kind. At the beginning of the period Antonio Bragadin* had agents at Aleppo and Tripoli and Zuan Francesco Priuli* had one at Istanbul; at the end of it Alvise Mocenigo* had agents at Istanbul. Two proctors from the Foscarini family (ai carmini branch) were definitely engaged in trade, Giacomo Foscarini* and his son Zuanbattista Foscarini,* who was active in both the oil and the timber business.[8] Polo Paruta* participated in the trade with Alexandria. Agostino Nani* and Zuanne Dolfin* were both involved in the trade with Syria.[9]

It is interesting to find two of these patricians, Antonio Bragadin* and Giacomo Foscarini,* arguing in their official capacities for the continuation of Venetian participation in the spice trade in 1584. In 1624 Antonio Grimani* had 12,000 ducats invested in a soapworks, and he exhorted his heirs to remain in the business. As for Zuanbattista Foscarini,* he was concerned not only with oil and timber but also in the trade in woollen cloth, which was of increasing importance in seventeenth-century Venice.

Foscarini* carried the business on through an agent, and the reliance on non-noble agents or partners seems to have been common among patricians. In 1660, for instance, Almoro Tiepolo* set up a company to trade in silk in partnership with Salamon Annobuono, a Jewish merchant.[10] In the later seventeenth century Domenico Contarini* had 2,000 ducats invested in a business with the Foscoli brothers, who were not nobles. Comparison with Amsterdam makes more obvious what the Venetians did not do – invest in joint-stock companies. The dominant form of business organization was still the family, even if in partnership with outsiders.

[8]   On A. Bragadin* and G. Foscarini,* Cervelli (1966).
[9]   Lowry (1971), 343, 354.
[10]   ASV, Archivio Notarile, busta 720, fo. 181. My thanks to Alex Cowan for this reference.

The elite can also be found trading in the produce of their estates, an activity practised by nobles in many parts of seventeenth-century Europe, from England to Russia. Nicolò Donà* was engaged in the grain trade; Zorzi Corner, the son of Zuan I Corner,* sold cattle and grain, Antonio Priuli* was in the timber business. Indeed, given the amount of land which was leased out by them for rents in kind, the majority of the elite must have engaged in this sort of trade, if only at second hand through a steward or manager.

Members of the elite also acquired their wealth by marriage and through the profits of office. In Venice, as elsewhere in early modern Europe, a wife came with a dowry. In the social group which we are discussing a dowry in this period might be anything from 5,000 to 200,000 ducats. The last figure is that of the dowry of Franceschina Dolfin, who married Girolamo, son of Antonio Priuli,* in 1618. To marry a daughter into the family of a reigning doge (as Priuli* was at the time) was an expensive business. One way of increasing the dowry was to marry below one's status, outside the Venetian nobility. Leaving aside the gossip that Doge Zuan Pesaro* had secretly married his housekeeper, we find that ten members of the elite married downwards during the period. Three married into newly ennobled families, the Labia and the Zenobio, while seven married commoners. For example, Zuanbattista Corner* married Zanetta Noris, whose family came from Brescia, while Benetto Soranzo* married a doctor's daughter, Maria Flangini.[11]

The profits of office might be ecclesiastical or secular. The ecclesiastical are better known. The philosopher Tommaso Campanella went so far as to say that 'the greater part of the nobility of Venice live from canonries and bishoprics'. He was making anti-Venetian propaganda and he was exaggerating, but he did have a point to exaggerate.[12] Some members of the elite retired from political life to enter the church, like Pietro Basadonna,* who became a cardinal, and Zuanne Dolfin,* who be-

[11] The ten cases are Molin*–Purperata (1576); Corner*–Noris (c.1625); Soranzo*–Flangini (1640); Grimani*–Bergonzi (1646); Foscarini*–Labia (1650); Contarini*–Tomi (1665); Ottobon*–Maretti (1665); Lando*–Zenobio (1668); Zen*–Pio (1692); Bragadin*–Zenobio (1697).
[12] Quoted in Ventura (1968), 677.

came cardinal and bishop of Vicenza. However, since in Venice a branch of a noble clan tended to pool its resources, one needs to look also at the benefices landed by the brothers, uncles and nephews of the elite.

Particularly successful in this respect were certain branches of the Grimani, Corner and Dolfin clans. It was said that the brothers Francesco Grimani,* Zuanbattista Grimani* and Zuan Grimani* were all supported by their relative the bishop of Bergamo.[13] Another bishop of Bergamo was Ferigo Corner, son of Doge Zuan I Corner,* while between 1577 and 1722 seven out of ten bishops of Padua came from the Corner clan.[14] From 1657 till well after the end of the period the archbishop of Udine was always a Dolfin.[15]

Historians have tended to place less emphasis on the possible profits of political office, but they were important too. The judicial offices of the *quarantia* were a well-known form of poor relief for impoverished noblemen. The offices held by members of the elite also included some with high salaries. In the early seventeenth century five senior naval officers received over 10,000 ducats each a year.[16] Ambassadors received from 5,000 to 7,000 ducats a year. It is true that these posts involved their holders in expenses, but it is equally true that over and above the salaries there were considerable perquisites and opportunities for profit. The difficult thing is to estimate this unofficial income. Official sources are naturally silent, while contemporary comment may well be exaggerated out of envy.

All the same, it seems worth recording that in the seventeenth century observers remarked on the 'modern alchemy' which was converting offices from a source of loss into a source of profit, and that it was said that in the war with the Habsburgs in 1617 some leading nobles enriched themselves with public money.[17] Indeed, the great Francesco Morosini* was twice accused, in 1663 and 1670, of keeping public money for himself.[18] One mid-seventeenth-century writer even drew up a list of the profits, as distinct from

13 EIP, 47.
14 Simioni (1968), 904.
15 Dolfin (1924), 163.
16 Relatione 3, fos 174ff.
17 EIP, 18; Relatione 2, fo. 143r.
18 Mosto (1960), 435.

the income, of offices, and mentioned among the most profitable the *governatori delle entrate*, supervising direct taxation; the *provveditori al sale*, administering the government's salt monopoly, an important form of indirect taxation; the *provveditore* of Corfu (worth about 12,000 ducats a year); and, most important of all, the *bailo* (ambassador) to Istanbul.[19] The *bailo* did not have to present accounts, although he was given money to bribe the grand vizier. One writer thought he might make 100,000 ducats in three years, or even more if he was greedy; another wrote that he was the only official 'who can rob without scruple'.[20]

After this general survey of the resources of the Venetian elite, it is time to ask whether they were entrepreneurs or rentiers in Pareto's sense of these terms. Of a small number, one can say with some confidence that they were entrepreneurs in the literal sense of being involved in trade and interested in profit; Antonio Bragadin,* Giacomo Foscarini* and Antonio Priuli* are examples who have already been quoted. Others, like Alvise da Mosto* and Ferigo Corner,* with considerable sums deposited in the Mint, can reasonably be classified as rentiers. Corner's* bequest in 1706 to 'my *fattore* in Venice . . . who knows about all my affairs' is another sign of his passive attitude to his wealth. All we know of the majority of the elite, however, is that they owned considerable amounts of land.

Owning land does not necessarily make a man a rentier (in the sense that the term is used throughout this book). What matters is a man's attitude to the land, whether active or passive, whether he is interested in 'projects of improvement' (as Adam Smith put it) or is content to sit back and wait for his steward to collect the rent. Some of the elite certainly had an active attitude to their land: Marcantonio Barbaro,* for example, owner of the famous Villa Maser, designed by Palladio and decorated by Veronese. Barbaro's* was a slightly unusual case in that he had virtually no property in Venice and virtually no other land. Of the 1,000 ducats a year which this estate brought him, according to his tax return, 60 per cent came from leasing it out and the high

[19]   Bacco (1856), 153ff.
[20]   RA, 393; Freschot (1709), 264.

proportion of 40 per cent from the direct administration of the demesne.

In 1550 a third of the mainland was uncultivated, and much was marshy, but around 1600 noble syndicates for draining the marshes were extremely active. Canals were dug and bridges were built. Much improvement was done by means of forced labour imposed on the local peasants by their Venetian rulers, the beneficiaries being the Venetian noble landowners, including some members of the elite.[21] Ferigo Contarini,* for instance, headed a consortium of nobles for the development of the area round Treviso. That he was interested in agriculture is also suggested by the fact that a certain Africo Clemente, notary of Padua, dedicated a treatise on the subject to him in 1572. Again, in the early seventeenth century Girolamo Corner* was involved in land reclamation.

In some cases one can watch individual members of the elite laying acre to acre. Luca Michiel* bought 69 *campi* of land at Meolo in 1607, and 11 more *campi* in 1610.[22] One unfriendly observer gave what one might call an 'imperialist' explanation of acquisitions like these, suggesting that the Venetian *rettori* 'skinned' the subject population of the mainland, and that Venetian nobles usurped the common lands and defrauded widows and orphans.[23] It is certainly the case that between 1646 and 1727 about 90,000 hectares of common land in the mainland was sold off, and that nearly 40 per cent of this amount was bought by Venetian nobles.[24]

There are instances where the documents give the impression that the elite were able to usurp the rights of others with impunity. Antonio Barbarigo* owned an estate at Casale, near Montagnana, in the Padua area. The commune complained that he had taken some of the common land 'on which we poor peasants are able to pasture our swine'. The case was heard by noble judges in Venice, and judgement given in Barbarigo's* favour in 1690, a year in which he held the office of *provveditore delli beni inculti*, con-

[21] Campos (1937), 15ff.
[22] BCV, Provenienze Diverse, s.v. 'Luca Michiel'.
[23] Relatione 2, fos 144ff.
[24] Beltrami (1961), 74ff.

cerned with uncultivated land in the *terraferma*. This looks like a
case of injustice, but after three hundred years it is obviously
difficult to be sure of the rights of the matter.[25]

It is also possible to find members of the elite with a relatively
passive or rentier attitude to their lands. Throughout the period
some of them employed managers or stewards to look after their
estates, as one might have expected, given the size of some estates
and the need for their owners to live in town most of the year for
political and other reasons. Africo Clemente, in his treatise on
agriculture (which went through eight Italian editions between
1572 and 1714), recommended Venetians to provide themselves
with 'skilled and experienced managers' (*fattori pratici et esperti*),
and to pay them well, insisting that they be professionals and not
servants used to other work such as looking after the horses. It is
likely that this advice was taken and that the seventeenth century
saw the increasing importance and professionalization of the
estate manager.

Evidence of such professionalization is the fact that a certain
Giacomo Agostinetti published a book of instructions for such
estate managers in 1679. The author boasts that he is a 'thorough-
bred steward' (*fattore di razza*), having served for forty-five years
in the Veneto, and his father having been a steward before him. He
is concerned with estates large enough to need a head steward with
subordinate bailiffs (*castaldi*) under him. He gives the impression
of highly rationalized estate management, singing the praises of
double-entry bookkeeping and recommending landowners to keep
coloured drawings of their estates with each piece numbered so
that they can visit their land without leaving Venice.

On the question of the control exercised by the owner,
Agostinetti is somewhat ambivalent. He suggests that the living
quarters in the villa should neither be too near the peasants, in
which case their noise may disturb the noble residents, nor too far,
or the owner will not be able to keep his eye on things. All the
same, he goes on to praise the Venetian senator who did not care
whether he bought land near Padua or near Treviso: 'It doesn't
matter to me whether my income comes to me along the Brenta or

[25] BCV, Provenienze Diverse, C.2347, busta 17.

along the Sile' – a rentier attitude if ever there was one. But then an entrepreneurial landowner would not have had much use for a steward.[26]

The wills of some members of the elite make references to stewards. Francesco Corner* (died 1584) had had his Cyprus estates administered by *fattori*, not altogether honestly. He recommended his heirs to look after the estates in person. On the other hand, Alvise Barbarigo* made a special bequest to the *fattore* of his villa at Merlana for good and faithful service. It must not be assumed, incidentally, that absentee landlords meant estates without improvements. The stewards of the Tron property at Anguillara near Padua in the mid eighteenth century reclaimed land and improved ploughing techniques.[27] If we compare the Venetians with other noble landowners in Europe, however, the absence of treatises on agriculture written by noblemen and of noble agricultural societies is remarkable.[28]

If it is not clear exactly how much interest members of the elite took in the details of estate management, it is still less clear how they treated their farm workers, who slept in the stables or lived in straw huts while their masters lived in palaces. The labour question is discussed in two treatises on agriculture written in the seventeenth century for noble landowners in the Veneto. G. B. Barpo, a voluble clergyman from Belluno, suggested that an estate would be a delight if it were not for the labourers, who were vicious, envious, proud and obstinate.[29] For his part, Agostinetti took a more moderate line. He knew that some of the tenants watered the wine or cheated in other ways, but recognized that others were reliable. Generosity on the landlord's part is a good investment: 'good landlords have good workers'. Agostinetti's attitude to the peasants is essentially manipulative. In one place in his book he discusses the choice of ploughs and the choice of tenants together; the peasant too was a tool.

One foreign visitor, the churchman Gilbert Burnet, claimed that 'In the Venetian territory . . . they oppress their tenants so severely

[26] Agostinetti (1679); cf. Ventura (1969).
[27] Georgelin (1968).
[28] Berengo (1956), 94.
[29] Barpo (1634), 26ff.

that the peasants live most miserably.'[30] He did not stay long enough in the region for his comments to be worth taking very seriously by themselves. However, another commentary on the Venetian noble landlord may be read by anyone who cares to browse through *Il Barbaro*, the famous Venetian collection of family trees with notes on the lives of individuals. Not infrequently one comes across the laconic entry 'murdered by the peasants' (*ammazzato da' contadini*).

In the case of Amsterdam, tax returns (*kohieren*) are again the best single source for examining the wealth of the elite, although the gaps between the assessments (made in 1585, 1631, 1674 and 1742) allow some extremely rich men to slip through the net, including Alexander Velters,* who left over 1 million florins when he died in 1719, and Jeronimus de Haze,* who left over 3 million when he died in 1725.[31] The tax was the 'two hundredth penny', in other words 5 per cent of property (replaced by an income tax in 1742). In 1585 65 individuals or households were assessed at 50 florins or more. Eighteen elite members, about half, belong to this group, and the men with the highest assessments in Amsterdam were burgomaster Dirck Graeff,* who paid 210 florins, and burgomaster Willem Baerdesen,* who paid 200 florins. In 1631 100 individuals or households were assessed at 500 florins or more, meaning that they were supposed to be worth 100,000 florins or more. Sixteen of these were members of the elite, and the largest fortune, 500,000 florins, was declared by the heirs of the late burgomaster Jacob Poppen.* In 1674 259 individuals or households were assessed at 500 florins or more; they included 35 members of the elite, of whom the richest was Joan Corver,* worth 419,000 florins. Seven years later he became burgomaster. In 1742 103 people declared an income of 16,000 florins or more, and 27 members of the elite belonged to this category. Burgomasters D. Trip,* J. Six* and L. Geelvinck* were the second-richest, third-richest and fifth-richest individuals respectively. To put all

[30]   Burnet (1686), 27.
[31]   For the *kohieren* of 1585, 1631 and 1742, see Dillen (1941), Frederiks and Frederiks (1890) and Oldewelt (1945); for that of 1674, see GA, Kohieren.

these figures in perspective, it may be worth adding that a skilled
worker earned about 200 florins a year at this time.[32]

Of course the historian cannot accept these tax returns at their
face value any more than tax returns in Venice or indeed anywhere
else. In a few cases the returns can be checked against other
sources – and found wanting. Jacob Poppen* left 920,000 florins
when he died in 1624, but his heirs were assessed at only 500,000
florins in 1631. Dirck Bas* was assessed at 100,000 florins in
1631, but left 500,000 florins in 1637. The 240,000 florins declared by E. Trip in 1674 were only 20 to 25 per cent of his real
wealth, according to a monograph on that family.[33]

On the other hand, some of the amounts which appear in the
returns may have been exaggerated. Andries de Graeff* was assessed at 292,000 florins in 1674. However, the assessment was
the work of his political enemies Gillis Valckenier* and Nicolaes
Witsen.* De Graeff* was aware of the danger and changed his
residence, moving to Utrecht to escape Amsterdam taxes, but this
device failed. Presumably it was a supporter of his faction who
stuck a paper on the Town Hall, inscribed 'Matthew 17.24–27'. St
Matthew says that 'Jesus asked Peter, of whom do the kings of the
earth take custom or tribute? Of their own children, or of strangers? Peter saith unto him, Of strangers. Jesus saith unto him,
Then are the children free.'[34]

Amsterdam tax records, unlike Venetian ones, do not say how
a man's wealth was made up. For this it is necessary to have
recourse to other kinds of source, notably the Registers of Collateral Succession (CS), since collateral heirs were subject to a 5 per
cent tax, which meant that the inheritance had to be described in
detail. From these sources it is clear that the Amsterdam elite
invested in houses, land, ships, stock and bonds. One result of the
great expansion of Amsterdam in the seventeenth century was the
inflation of the price of houses, which were often divided among
several owners. Thus Josias van de Blocquery* owned 5/32 of a
house in Amsterdam. Houses were a safe but not enormously

---

[32]   Méchoulan (1993), 83.
[33]   P. W. Klein (1965).
[34]   Bontemantel (1897), vol. 2, 107ff.

profitable investment. One estimate, in 1622, was that they brought in 3 per cent per annum.[35]

Land also brought in the safe but slender profit of 3 per cent per annum.[36] About 30 per cent of the elite appear to have owned some land, but it is not altogether clear what the land was used for. The pattern seems to differ in each of the few cases where some of the details are known. Joannes Hudde* was described as a 'cattle breeder' (ossenweider). All the same, he did not own very much land, just over 4,000 florins' worth. The biggest piece was about 15 morgen of land near Sloterdijk, just outside Amsterdam, which had peasant houses on it. Did the peasants look after his cattle?[37] Fredrik Willem van Loon* had a farm, Treslong, but also small pieces of land which seem to have been rented out as 'residences'.[38] Marten van Loon's* land, unlike the others, carried manorial rights. Jacob de Graeff* had his manor of Zuidpolsbroek administered by a steward (drossard, rentmeester). It is not clear whether this practice was a general one.[39]

A third possible investment, popular in the late sixteenth and early seventeenth centuries, was in voyages, that is, in trading ventures.[40] For instance, when Cornelisz Joriszoon* married Grietge Backer in 1588, he was worth 24,000 florins, of which 2,000 was invested in voyages.[41] In the early seventeenth century, with the rise of the VOC, this form of investment was replaced by stock (actiën). Stock was not a safe investment in a period and a city when speculation on the Stock Exchange was already a fine art, but there was the possibility of enormous profits. When Admiral Piet Hein captured the Spanish silver fleet in 1628, the WIC paid a dividend of 50 per cent. As for the VOC, its success may be measured from the fact that at his death in 1722 Nicolaas van Bambeeck* held 'old stock' of the VOC of which the face value was 21,000 florins; its true value was assessed at 146,000 florins.[42]

[35] G. W. Kernkamp (1897), 29.
[36] CS, vol. 19, fo. 300.
[37] CS, vol. 16, fo. 482.
[38] CS, vol. 13, fo. 158.
[39] GA, de Graeff papers, no. 43.
[40] H. A. E. van Gelder (1918), 29ff.
[41] GA, Backer papers, no. 63.
[42] CS, vol. 18, fo. 1156.

There was also the possibility of enormous losses. To decrease the risk, owners of stock distributed their holdings between different companies and different chambers of the same company. Alexander Velters,* for example, held stock in the VOC (Amsterdam chamber) and the WIC (Amsterdam chamber) and also in the Delft and Enkhuizen chambers of the VOC.[43] Jeronimus de Haze* invested in the English South Sea Company as well as in Dutch companies.[44]

A fourth form of investment was in bonds (*obligatiën*), that is, in loans, usually to the city of Amsterdam or the province of Holland. In 1622 this was said to bring in 5 or 6 per cent a year, nearly twice as much as houses or land; but in 1679 Amsterdam was paying only 4 per cent interest.[45] The VOC also borrowed money in this way. An alternative method of investment in the public debt was the purchase of *rentebrieven*, or annuities, which could be bought and sold like stock. One kind of annuity – the *losrente brief* – was specifically redeemable. Another kind was the life annuity, which expired on the death of the holder.[46]

It is obviously important to know in what proportions the wealth of the Amsterdam elite was distributed between these four forms of investment. Unfortunately, it is possible to give a precise answer to this question only in a small number of cases, and most of them (fifteen, to be exact) are from the early eighteenth century. From these cases it appears that a typical investment pattern for a member of the elite about the year 1700 would have been to invest about half his wealth in bonds, about 32 per cent in stock, 12 per cent in houses and 6 per cent in land. More scattered pieces of evidence from the early seventeenth century suggest that about the year 1600 land was a much more important form of investment, accounting for some 30 per cent of wealth. Bonds were much less important. Shares were held in specific voyages of specific ships. (For the evidence on which this paragraph is based, see the appendix.)

Since they were not noblemen, members of the Amsterdam elite were often described by occupation, so that it is possible to say

---

[43]   CS, vol. 18, fo. 61.
[44]   CS, vol. 19, fo. 1017.
[45]   GA, Vroedschap, Resolutiën, vol. 33, 4ff.
[46]   Houtzager (1950).

something about how they made their money as well as how they invested it. Contemporary occupational descriptions of the Town Council were collected by J. E. Elias. Nearly half were described as merchants of some kind, including herring-merchants, like Cornelisz Joriszoon,* Gerrit Delft* or Claes van Vlooswijck.* This was a traditional Amsterdam occupation, like timber-merchant (Harmen van de Poll* and his son Jan van de Poll*), rope-merchant (Pieter Boom,* Jan Verburch*), soapboiler, like various members of the Spiegel family, or brewer, the occupation in which the Bickers made their money.

Around the year 1600 these occupations were the dominant ones, but then the pattern began to change.[47] Some members of the elite were quick to move into the new, dangerous and profitable trade with the Indies. Gerrit Bicker* was moving from brewing into the East Indies trade before his death in 1604, while Hendrick Hudde* was already involved in this trade as early as 1594. A third of the elite were directors of the VOC or the WIC or the Society of Surinam.

Towards the end of the period banking became an important occupation, or at least part-time banking combined with trade, as in the case of Balthasar Scott* and his father Everard Scott,* Daniel Hochepied* and Jean Deutz.* Printing and bookselling became important in Amsterdam in the course of the seventeenth century, and the king of Amsterdam printers was surely Dr Joan Blaeu,* whose press on the Bloemgracht was the largest and most up to date in Europe. He was map-maker to the VOC, and also involved in the shipping of slaves to the plantations of Virginia.[48]

Fourteen members of the elite were described either as 'seller of dairy produce' (*zuivelkooper*) or 'stockbreeder' (*ossenweider*). One might call them entrepreneur landowners. Stock-breeding meant importing lean cattle from the Holstein area, fattening them and selling them to feed the growing population of Amsterdam – an occupation which was increasing in importance, if we can argue from the fact that in 1660 the market for Danish cattle was moved from Enkhuizen to Amsterdam.[49] This group includes

[47] Ravesteyn (1906), 272.
[48] Koeman (1970), 10.
[49] Nielsen (1933), 141, 166.

Balthasar Appelman* and Joannes Hudde.* If it is added to the merchants, then the two together would include over half of the elite. Another form of entrepreneurship was participation in land-drainage schemes, notably the draining of the Purmer and the Beemster. Of the sixteen original head-landholders (*hoofd-ingelanden*) of the Beemster in 1608, four were members of the elite: Pieter Boom,* Barthold Cromhout,* Jan ten Grootenhuis* and Jacob Poppen.* This spectacular and profitable undertaking (most remarkable for the use of windmills in a land-drainage scheme) may help explain how Jacob Poppen* and others (p. 62 above) owned as much land as they did.[50]

Thirty, or just under 10 per cent, of the Amsterdam elite were professional men: lawyers in the main, like the three advocates who came from a single family, Cornelis Cloeck,* Nanning Cloeck* and Pieter Cloeck,* and also a few doctors, Martin Coster* and Nicolaes Tulp* being the most famous examples. Another was Jan van Hartoghvelt,* for whom his political opponents once arranged a sick-call so that he would miss a crucial meeting of the Council. There were also some naval officers, of whom the best known is Jacob van Neck.* Thirty-nine of the elite were directors of companies but not described as merchants or lawyers; it is difficult to know whether to see them as businessmen or bureaucrats.

The most striking feature of this brief survey is surely that, although the Amsterdam elite were defined in the first instance by political criteria, more than half of them have turned out to have been concerned with trade, and a third to have been connected with the East and West India Companies. There can be little doubt of the connection between the economic basis of the elite and some of their political attitudes. There are powerful individuals of whom one might say, not unfairly, adapting a phrase of Charles Wilson (the American secretary of state, not the British historian), that they behaved as if the business of the United Provinces was business and as if what was good for the VOC was good for the Dutch Republic. The ties between business, politics and war were even closer than the ties C. Wright Mills found in the 'power elite'

[50] Bouman (1856–7), 263ff.

of the USA in the time of the Korean war. The munitions manufacturers on the Amsterdam Town Council included Reynier Cant,*
Louys Trip* and Gillis Sautijn* (the last two, inserted by
Stadholder William III, favoured his war policy when the majority
of the Town Council favoured peace). Abraham Boom* and Jan
Geelvinck* sold ships to Spain in the early seventeenth century,
while Andries Bicker* supplied silver to Spain which was used to
pay Spanish troops in the Netherlands. No wonder the Town
Council commented in 1607 that peace would be the ruin of 'these
lands'.[51]

The last question to ask about the economic basis of the Amsterdam elite is whether they were rentiers or entrepreneurs. Sev-
enty-seven members of the elite, or just under 25 per cent, appear
to have had no occupation at all. It is obviously dangerous to
build an argument on the lack of surviving contemporary occupational descriptions, but in a number of cases we also have
positive evidence that these men were what their contemporaries
called *renteniers*, men who lived from the interest on their bonds.
These 'renteeners' (as Sir William Temple translated the Dutch
term) are classic cases of what we call 'rentiers'. They included
Fredrik Willem van Loon,* Jacob Bicker* and Nicolaas van
Bambeeck.*

In other cases, it is harder to classify individuals as rentiers or
entrepreneurs because in the wide sense in which the terms are
being used here, attitudes are as important as investments. Burgomaster F. H. Oetgens,* for instance, owned a good deal of urban
property. A man who lives on the rent of houses looks like a
rentier, but in fact Oetgens* was an expert and unscrupulous
speculator in real estate. He was *stadsfabriekmeester* of Amsterdam, planning urban development. He bought land outside the
city walls near the Haarlem Gate, and then planned the expansion
of the city in just that direction, so that his property increased
greatly in value. C. P. Hooft* protested against what Oetgens*
was doing, and wanted the city to take over the land, but Oetgens*
was able to hold on to his gains.[52] No wonder an Amsterdam wit
called part of the city 'Jordaan', 'the promised land', and the name

---

[51]　Brugmans (1897–1905), 61.
[52]　N. de Roever (1889), 66ff.

stuck. Again, Jacob Poppen* with his investments in land looks like a rentier, but he was very much involved in a project for improvement, the draining of the Beemster. Paradoxically enough, it looks as though the Amsterdam elite were most entrepreneurial in attitude when they were most involved with land, in the early seventeenth century, and that the retreat from land into bonds and the rise of 'rentier' attitudes occurred together.

To sum up: the one thing which it ought to be possible to compare precisely in the two cities is wealth, but it is in fact difficult to say which of the two groups was the richer. The problem is not that of converting ducats into florins, which is easy enough, at least after the foundation of the Amsterdam Exchange in 1609. In 1609 a ducat was worth about 2.5 florins, declining to about 2 florins by 1718.[53] The real difficulty is that of comparing information about income in Amsterdam, derived from the *kohier* of 1674, with information about property in Venice, derived from the *decima* of 1711.

A plausible estimate of the average wealth of a member of the Venetian elite in 1711 would be 150,000 ducats, which can be converted into 300,000 florins. For a comparable estimate of the wealth of the Amsterdam elite, it is necessary to go back to 1675. The average wealth of a member of the elite was then 167,000 florins, not much more than half the wealth of his Venetian opposite number – a surprising conclusion for the late seventeenth century, when Amsterdam was at its peak and Venice in decline.

Other comparisons are both vaguer and simpler. According to the broad definition of 'rentier' and 'entrepreneur' as contrasted psychological and economic types, Venice seems to have been predominantly rentier (with some entrepreneurs) while Amsterdam was predominantly entrepreneur (with quite a few rentiers). In both places there was a shift from entrepreneur to rentier during the seventeenth century, a shift which will be the subject of a later chapter. With this major contrast other differences are associated. Land was an important investment in Amsterdam but non-existent in Venice. Venice may have been colonialist in north Italy, but Venetians missed out on the much more profitable colonialism in the Indies.

[53] Posthumus (1943–64), vol. 1, 590ff.

In a significant number of Venetian instances the profits of office were an important means of acquiring wealth. This source was relatively unimportant in Amsterdam, except perhaps in the case of the *schout*, or sheriff (about 1650 his official income was 500 florins, but his unofficial income was more like 6,000 florins).[54] The profits of politics were more indirect in Amsterdam. They consisted essentially of influencing the foreign policy of the Dutch Republic in the direction Amsterdam businessmen desired. To treat politics as a source of profit was natural in the seventeenth century, however it may shock the modern European reader. It may make comprehension of this fact, by no means confined to Venice and Amsterdam, somewhat easier if the reader remembers that politics was also a source of loss, and that some men ruined themselves to live in the style demanded by the political offices they held. The style of life and the spending patterns of the two elites form the subject of the next chapter.

[54]   G. W. Kernkamp (1897), 100.

5

Style of Life

From the making and investing of wealth we now turn to the ways in which the two elites consumed it, and to the way of life which this spending made possible. Each of the two groups had, besides their distinctive attitudes and values, to be described in the next chapter, their own customary ways of walking, talking, working or relaxing, formed by training children to imitate a particular ideal.

The Venetian style was the style of a nobility, who used coats of arms and were fascinated by genealogy (*Il Barbaro*, a compilation of the family trees of the whole Venetian nobility, was begun in the later sixteenth century). The proctors were a kind of higher nobility. They wore special purplish or bluish costumes (*paonazzo* was the contemporary term), with sleeves trailing the ground, which set them off from other nobles. The election of a new proctor was followed by a splendid rite of passage, with trumpets blowing, cannon firing, the portrait of the successful candidate displayed in the streets, the distribution of bread, wine and money to the people and a procession from the Church of San Salvador to the Church of San Marco.

In other ways the Venetians were, by European standards, a most unusual nobility. Their long black gowns made it clear that they belonged to the robe rather than the sword. Despite the fact that some of them had distinguished naval careers, they were essentially civilians. Unlike their colleagues all over Europe,

Venetian nobles did not normally wear swords in public. Like Chinese mandarins, whom they resembled in more than one way, they were poor riders. In the fifteenth century the Florentine humanist Poggio Bracciolini recorded a joke about a Venetian who was unable to recognize his own horse.[1] Horses were of course as useless in this city of canals as cars are today, and in 1608 the English traveller Thomas Coryat noted: 'I saw but one horse in all Venice during the space of six weeks that I made my abode there.'[2]

Equally unusual for a nobility, the traditional Venetian style of life was one of frugality rather than display. Doge Lunardo Donà* is perhaps a good example to take, because in the early seventeenth century he was seen by contemporaries as a model Venetian nobleman. Donà* was thrifty to the point of avarice. He told his heirs to live simply, and he even bought his carriage second-hand.[3] Again, when Zuan Sagredo* was ambassador at Paris, so the contemporary story went, he would come back from audience with the King and tell his footmen to take off their liveries, to save wear and tear.[4] Coryat commented on the nobility in general that 'they keep no honourable hospitality, nor gallant retinue of servants about them, but a very frugal table', despite the wealth of some of them. He remarked on the fact that noblemen could be seen buying food in the markets themselves, which he thought beneath the dignity of their status.[5] This traditional ideal of frugality was encouraged by the sumptuary laws issued by the *provveditori alle pompe,* the 'overseers of displays'. Sumptuary laws were common enough in seventeenth-century Europe, but it was unusual to apply them to the nobility. Yet in 1658, for example, noble Venetians were forbidden to eat off silver plates and guests at banquets were forbidden to eat more than one and a half pounds of marzipan at a sitting.[6]

Gravity and dignity were valued highly by Venetian nobles. Their robes forced them to walk in a slow and dignified manner

[1] Bracciolini (1880).
[2] Coryat (1611), vol. 1, 364.
[3] Cutolo (1953), 278;　cf. Davis (1975), 37–41.
[4] RA, 414.
[5] Coryat (1611), vol. 1, 415, 397.
[6] Bistort (1912), esp. 414–67.

and the use of the gondola made their progress that much more stately.[7] Some members of the elite were particularly conspicuous for their dignity. It was noted, for instance, that Doge Francesco Morosini* would never cross his legs in public.[8] Nicolò Corner* was described as having a 'fine presence' (bellissima presenza) and a royal manner.[9] Ceremoniousness was also part of the Venetian style. Coryat noticed that Venetian nobles 'give a low congie to each other by very civil and courteous gestures, as by bending of their bodies and clapping their right hand upon their breasts', while a French visitor commented on the habit of kissing a man's sleeve as a greeting.[10] This cultural style was formed by the juniors imitating their seniors, for the doge and the proctors were usually old men. Of the twenty-five doges elected between 1578 and 1720, the average age at election was sixty-seven. In any case, as Fynes Moryson, an English gentleman who visited Venice in 1594, perceptively observed, Venetians were prematurely old, or more exactly 'rather seem than truly be aged'.[11] Where else but in Venice could they call the group led by Donà* the 'youngsters' (giovani)? Donà* was forty-six in 1582 and seventy when he was elected doge.

Another ingredient of the Venetian cultural style was an emphasis on silence. The late-sixteenth-century allegorical paintings in the Doge's Palace included not only Fame and Victory but also Taciturnity.[12] Lunardo Donà* wrote a note to himself, 'don't be loquacious' (non esser loquace). A studied inscrutability was the ideal. As Fra Paolo Sarpi once wrote of Dona,* 'One never knows whether he loves or hates anything.'[13] It was not only at Carnival that Venetians wore masks. An interest in simulation and dissimulation was common among the elites of seventeenth-century Europe, but it seems to have been particularly intense among Venetian patricians, and may owe something to the broglio, their informal political meetings on Piazza San Marco (p. 79 below).

---

[7] On the history of Italian gesture, Burke (1991a).
[8] Mosto (1960), 435.
[9] RA, 399.
[10] Coryat (1611), vol. 1, 399; Misson (1691–8), vol. 1, 196.
[11] Moryson (1907–8), vol. 1, 164.
[12] Bardi (1587), fo. 30. On the history of silence, Burke (1993a).
[13] Seneca (1959), 37.

Antonino Colluraffi, a private tutor in Venice, advised nobles at the *broglio* to penetrate the thoughts of others 'in order to accommodate oneself the better to their humours' (*per potessi a'loro humori più agevolmente conformare*).[14] Antonio Ottobon* advised his son to model himself on Proteus and please everyone by being all things to all men (*Tu dovrai qual Proteo mutar figure per renderti grato ad ognuno*). A less friendly observer suggested that Venetian noblemen 'dissimulate a great deal among themselves, and however greatly they might hate someone, they always put on a friendly face'.[15] If contemporaries found them difficult to understand, the twentieth-century historian of the Venetian nobility had better beware of overconfidence.

The noble Venetian style of life was marked by frugality, by gravity and by prudence. Its dominant note was self-control. The local ethos discouraged eating, drinking, talking and spending money in excess of requirements. Lunardo Donà* added to this a vow of chastity, and of Nicolò Contarini* it was said that he died a virgin. The individual patrician was expected to suppress his desires and even his personality for the sake of his family and his city. 'I should like to be known in the Roman curia as ambassador of Venice . . . and not as Lunardo Donà; and equally in Venice as senator of that fatherland . . . and not by my private name.'[16] At a time when it was increasingly common to erect statues in public places representing the holders of high office, the Venetian government set its face against this cult of personality. In 1623, for example, the Senate intervened to forbid the erection of a statue of the Governor of Belluno on the piazza of that city.[17] Whether it should be described modesty or avarice, this attitude extended beyond the grave. Donà* asked his heirs to spend only 500 ducats on his monument. A number of the elite declare in their wills that they want to be buried without any pomp (unusual for a seventeenth-century noble) and Ferigo Contarini* went so far as to enforce his wishes on his heirs with a penalty of 10,000 ducats.

In 1617 a certain Carlos García published a book on the contrast between the Spaniards and the French, including their ways

[14] Colluraffi (1623–33), vol. 1, ch. 19.
[15] Amelot (1676), 338.
[16] Bouwsma (1968), 234.
[17] Chambers and Pullan (1992), 410.

of dressing, drinking, walking and speaking. The book was soon translated into Italian and, to judge by the number of editions, enjoyed considerable success there.[18] It was probably thanks to García that an anonymous seventeenth-century observer of Venice described the traditional style of life, and its gravity and ceremoniousness in particular, as a 'Spanish' style (*genio spagnuolo*). However, this observer also noted the existence of a rival 'French' style, more open, more flamboyant, more generous, more relaxed.[19] Francesco Contarini,* for instance, was a man with a 'gentle manner' (*dolce maniera*).[20] Another anonymous observer described Nicolò Corner* in the same vein as friendly and even 'jovial' and Piero Dolfin* as gay, pleasant and full of promises which he did not keep.[21] In similar fashion, Doge Domenico Contarini* impressed a French visitor by his *douceur* and his *affabilité*.[22]

In short, the traditional life-style of Venetian patricians was changing in the course of the seventeenth century. Even horseriding was becoming more popular among young noblemen in the period. A joust was organized at Padua in 1600 by the *podestà* and the *capitano*. Riding academies spread on the mainland in the early seventeenth century, and from about 1600 onwards there was a riding-school in Venice itself, La Cavallerizza, at the Mendicanti.[23] Conspicuous consumption seems to have been increasing at more or less the same time.[24]

Among Venetian nobles, an ideal of personal frugality coexisted with an emphasis on public splendour, for the honour of the family or the honour of the state, *il publico decoro*, as Francesco Erizzo once described it.[25] Domenico Contarini* referred in his will to the 'luxury' necessary to keep up the style of a doge (*sostener si gran grado*). There is evidence of this stress on public splendour no matter what the expense throughout the period. For example, when King Henri III of France visited Venice in 1574, he

18 García (1617).
19 EIP, *passim*.
20 EIP, 49.
21 RA, 399, 374.
22 Saint-Didier (1680), 180.
23 Hale (1973).
24 Burke (1982).
25 Borgherini-Scarabellin (1917), 12.

was entertained magnificently by Ferigo Contarini* in his villa at Mira on the Brenta; and when the minor German prince Ernst August visited Venice in 1685, he was entertained with similar magnificence by Marco Contarini* in his villa at Piazzola. The host even organized a mock naval battle in the grounds of the villa, as well as paying for a publication describing the festivities.[26]

Conspicuous consumption was becoming a duty for holders of high political office. Marin Grimani* spent 6,943 ducats on the celebrations when he was elected doge in 1595 (it was of course characteristic of a Venetian nobleman to record his expenses so precisely). To serve as a governor on the mainland might also be costly. Andrea Contarini* refers in his will to the 'enormous expense' involved when he was *rettore* at Udine, while a contemporary remarked on the 'splendour' with which Zuanbattista Corner* served as *provveditore* of Peschiera and *capitano* of Bergamo in the 1640s.[27] Another expensive office was *capitano generale da mar*.

Most expensive of all, in all probability, was the office of ambassador. Indeed, it was not unknown for a man's enemies to intrigue to have him appointed ambassador in order to ruin him.[28] Nicolò Corner* was said to have spent 20,000 ducats in a few days on an extraordinary embassy to the Emperor. This figure should not be taken too seriously, but in the case of one extraordinary embassy to the Emperor, undertaken by Anzolo Contarini* and Renier Zen,* an itemized expense account has survived.[29] The journey there and back cost them 2,500 ducats. This included the cost of transporting and feeding their retinue, plus incidental expenses like tips to trumpeters, alms to churches on the route and the painting of shields to leave behind at the inns where they stayed. All the same, 2,500 ducats was a great deal to spend in a few days, and an ordinary ambassador held his post for about three years. It is no wonder that at the end of the seventeenth century it was sometimes difficult to find nobles who would accept the appointment. Alvise Pisani,* for instance, was appointed am-

[26]   Piccioli (1685).
[27]   EIP, 63ff.
[28]   RA, 391.
[29]   BCV, MS Cicogna 2538.

bassador to France in 1698 after four previous candidates had refused. Being a Pisani of Santo Stefano, he could afford it.

The Amsterdam elite had no such conscious traditional style, perhaps because they belonged not to an estate but to a class, not to a formal but to an informally defined group. It is true that some of them were knighted, as a result of missions abroad. Reynier Pauw,* for example, was knighted by both James I and Louis XIII, and Dirck Bas* by Gustav Adolf, while Willem Backer* became a knight of San Marco at Venice in 1647. Some members of the elite bought country estates with titles attached. Jacob de Graeff* became Vrijheer van Zuidpolsbroek after buying this estate from the Prince of Aremberg in 1610. Cornelis Bicker* became Heer van Swieten after buying the estate of Swieten, near Leiden, in 1632. Joan Huydecoper* became Heer van Marsseveen in similar fashion in 1640.

By the early seventeenth century a few members of the elite can already be found compiling family trees and trying to prove noble descent. Gerard Schaep* scoffed at another patrician for 'the vainglory of his family tree' (*die ydele glorie van sijn geslacht-boom*), but his papers survive to show that he believed his own family descended from the Silesian nobility.[30] Andries de Graeff* claimed descent from the von Graben, a noble family from the Tyrol. However, this group within the elite (probably a small minority at the time), was not formally distinct from the rest. No one could have listed the patricians of Amsterdam in the way that the golden book listed the patricians of Venice.

The Amsterdam elite wore no official robes like the doge, proctors or senators of Venice. On official occasions they wore the same black gowns or coats as professional men and businessmen usually wore. Their movements were not particularly ceremonious. Although they lived on canals, they did not glide in gondolas but walked the streets like everyone else. The British envoy Henry Sidney remarked with surprise that burgomaster Gillis Valckenier* 'walks about without a footman': 'He walks about

30 GA, Bicker papers, no. 717.

the street just like an ordinary shopkeeper.'[31] Another British diplomat, Sir William Temple, generalized the point when he wrote that the burgomasters of Amsterdam 'are obliged to no sort of expense, more than ordinary modest citizens, in their habits, their attendance, their tables'. On the contrary, they 'appear in all places with the simplicity and modesty of other private citizens'.[32] This point struck the Venetians too. Tommaso Contarini, on a mission to the Dutch Republic in 1610, was impressed by the simple style of life there, which he thought the Venetians had not equalled even in earlier centuries.[33] Other sources, such as household accounts, confirm the picture of a relatively simple life-style even among the wealthier regents, with particularly little being spent on servants.[34]

The Amsterdam style does seem to have become somewhat grander during the period. Nicolaes Tulp* attacked sumptuous wedding feasts and had a law against them passed in 1655. This did not stop Louys Trip* from spending 8,300 florins on the wedding of his daughter Anna Maria to Wouter Valckenier* in 1670 (money well spent, for this alliance helped him enter the Town Council in 1672). The famous Trippenhuis in Amsterdam was another example of conspicuous consumption. A French visitor reported the rumour that it had cost more than 400,000 florins.

In the eighteenth century these changes went still further. They can be illustrated from the tax assessments of 1742, when information was collected about such status symbols as country houses, coaches and horses. Country houses grew bigger in the eighteenth century and imitated the French style more closely. Costume also symbolized an important change in the style of life of the Dutch regents as a whole. In the seventeenth century they wore sober black. In the eighteenth century, in contrast, they had themselves painted in coloured clothes, as in the case of a famous group portrait by Cornelis Troost, now in the Rijksmuseum. Self-control seems to have been less of a virtue than it had been in the seventeenth century.

---

[31]   Sidney (1843), vol. 1, 64.
[32]   Temple (1673), 59ff.
[33]   Blok (1909), 38.
[34]   Muinck (1967).

Of course there were variations within the two groups as well as differences between them. The Venetians included a bluff sea-dog like Francesco da Molin,* known for his hard drinking and his rough direct way of speaking, as well as Pietro Basadonna,* 'a cunning, polished courtier' (scaltro e raffinato cortigiano), who was always smiling in his sardonic way.[35] Differences like these were not just differences between individual temperaments, but differences of cultural style associated with differences in social role. The Venetian elite, which monopolized power in the whole state, needed naval officers like da Molin* as well as diplomats like Basadonna.* In Amsterdam there was less spectacular variety because there was less need for variety. Amsterdammers were in the main a group of merchants, and the bulk of Dutch diplomats and naval officers came from elsewhere. C. P. Hooft* and Reynier Pauw* differed very greatly in attitudes, but not very much in their style of life.

Unlike most European nobilities of the seventeenth century (with the exception of the French noblesse de robe), the elites of both Amsterdam and Venice were essentially urban groups. In Venice the main residence of each branch of the clan was the palace in town, not the villa or villas on the mainland. The branch might take its name from the part of Venice in which the palace was situated, like the Foscarini ai carmini, in the parish of the Carmelite church, or the Grimani ai servi, in the parish of the Servites. It was the town palace on which most money was spent, and the town palace where the branch spent most of the year. The elite had to stay in town for political reasons. The state was governed from the Doge's Palace, the meeting-place of the Greater Council, the Senate, the College and the Council of Ten. The doge was not allowed to leave Venice without permission. Other nobles could leave whenever they wanted, but the Senate usually met every Saturday (much more often in times of crisis) and the Greater Council every Sunday morning.

Of course a council with some two thousand members could not do all its business in one morning a week. Hence the crucial importance of another urban institution, the broglio (thanks to which this Italian word has changed its meaning from 'garden' to

[35] RA, 384.

'intrigue'). Foreign visitors noticed that Piazza San Marco and its piazzetta were full of nobles 'in great troops' every day between five and eight in the evening. It was here that the higher nobility paid court to the lower, soliciting their votes for the following Sunday. A political market-place, as more than one visitor re-marked, but one where business was done with great ceremony and deep bows.[36] Indeed, if a noble did not bow low enough, he was said to be 'stiff-backed' (duro di schiena) and had trouble getting what he wanted. To be successful in politics it was neces-sary to cultivate one's superiors, equals and inferiors, to know not only their names but also their families, their alliances and their place in the system of political patrons and clients.[37]

Piazza San Marco was an important part of what the anthro-pologist Erving Goffman has called the 'front' for the self-presen-tation of the Venetian nobles.[38] It was the stage on which they acted, with the common people and the foreign visitors as the spectators. On this stage they learned the arts of simulation and dissimulation, described earlier in this chapter. Other incentives for the Venetian nobility to stay in town in autumn and winter were the carnival and the opera, to be discussed below. It was also in town that two important leisure institutions of the nobility were located: the gambling saloon and the academy.

In the sixteenth century gambling had taken the form of bets on elections to the Greater Council. This was forbidden by the government, and in the seventeenth century gambling took the politically more innocuous form of playing cards for money in public rooms (ridotti) provided for the purpose. Among the enthusiasts for this activity were Bertucci Valier,* Daniele IV Dolfin,* Silvestro Valier* and Giacomo Correr,* who spent his winnings paying his fines for refusing political office. No doubt their studied inscrutability was an asset to patrician gamblers.[39]

As for the academy, by the seventeenth century it was not an informal group of friends (as it had been in the early Renaissance) but a club, with a fixed meeting-place, 'protectors' and a 'device' (impresa).[40] Academies were organized by nobles, though com-

---

[36] Amelot (1676), 17; Saint-Didier (1680), 35.
[37] Colluraffi (1623–33), vol. 1, ch. 19.
[38] Goffman (1959), 22ff.
[39] Colluraffi (1623–33), vol. 1, ch. 21; Molmenti (1879), vol. 5, 170ff.
[40] Battagia (1826); Quondam, (1982).

moners might be invited to join. The Delphic Academy, for example, met in the palace of Senator Francesco Gussoni. Its protectors were Zuanbattista Corner* and Alvise Duodo.* Its device was a tripod, with the motto 'from here the oracle' (hinc oracula). Cristoforo Ivanovitch, a well-known minor poet, was one of the commoners who were members.[41]

Two of the best-known academies of the period were the Cacciatrice (Huntress) and the Incogniti (Unknown ones'). The Cacciatrice, which flourished around the year 1600, met in the palace of Senator Andrea Morosini. The Renaissance philosopher Giordano Bruno expounded his views there. Its members included Nicolò Contarini,* Lunardo Donà* and, among the commoners, Paolo Sarpi, the famous Servite friar, polymath and historian of the Council of Trent. It was a convention that during meetings members 'did not stand on ceremony' with one another.[42]

As for the Incogniti, they were founded by Zuanfrancesco Loredan and met in his palace. Its members quite literally came incognito: they wore masks. This at once solved the problem of ceremony in a mixed gathering of nobles and commoners, and made it possible for members like the famous 'libertine' Ferrante Pallavicino to express unorthodox religious views without fear of the consequences – there were informers and inquisitors in seventeenth-century Venice. Women were allowed to attend the meetings, which had an erotic, frivolous yet learned atmosphere not unlike that of a Paris salon of the period. The academy discussed such topics as the value of ugliness, why A is the first letter of the alphabet and why Pythagoras objected to beans.[43]

Despite these activities in the city, Venetian patricians enjoyed prolonged visits to their villas in the country. The most popular place to have a villa was along the river Brenta. Many of these villas, more or less dilapidated, are still visible today. Villas were farms – the importance of land to the Venetian elite has already been discussed – but they were also holiday residences. Thus Domenico Contarini* referred to a visit to his villa at Valnogaredo 'to take a little relaxation in those hills of ours', while Agostino

[40] Battagia (1826); Quondam (1982).
[41] Sansovino (1663), 396.
[42] Favaro (1893).
[43] Lupis (1663), 17; Loredan (1635, 1676).

Nani* built a villa at Monselice with an entrance arch over which was the inscription 'You are off duty here; take off your robes' (*Emeritam hic, suspende togam*).[44] The 'ebb and flow' of the nobles along the Brenta was an event as regular as the tides. The summer season for *villeggiatura*, as it was called, began on 12 June and ended with the end of July. The autumn season began on 4 October and ended in mid-November. For its owner and his friends the villa was a refuge from politics. In it he could study or drive away the almost inevitable boredom with chess or cards, parlour games or practical jokes.[45] Near the villa he could shoot hares or go fowling in a boat with a bow and pellets of terracotta – even when he hunted, the Venetian nobleman did not mount a horse. For a view of these villas as they appeared at the end of the period, one may turn to the celebratory publication by Vincenzo Coronelli: *The Brenta, Land of Delight for the Venetian Patricians* (1709).[46]

Amsterdam patricians were still more of an urban group than Venetian ones. They tended to congregate along a few canals. The most popular, for members of the elite, were the Herengracht and the Keizersgracht, which look today much as they did in 1700. For political reasons they needed to be within easy reach of the Town Hall, where the burgomasters, councillors and magistrates all had their chambers. There was no *broglio* in Amsterdam, no Greater Council to court, no need to formalize the process of intrigue and bargaining. But the regents needed to stay in town to be within easy reach of the Bourse, East India House, West India House and the harbour itself. This was why to be sent even as far as The Hague was exile for an Amsterdam patrician.

The Amsterdam elite were not entirely urban either. They too had their country estates and their villas, or shares in villas (at least a third of the group): farms (*hofsteden*), country places (*buitenplaatsen*), pleasure-houses (*lusthuizen*) or play-houses (*speelhuizen*), they called them, where they could follow the advice of the poet Horace and devote themselves to leisure (*otium*) rather than business (*negotium*). The poems in praise of rural life by

[44]   F. Nani Mocenigo (1894), 164.
[45]   Sagredo (1655); Molmenti (1879), vol. 5, 181ff.
[46]   Coronelli (1709); Piovene and Magagnato (1960). Cf. Mazzotti (1953, 1957).

members of the regent class such as Constantijn Huygens and
Jacob Cats show that they were well aware of this classical ideal.
This aspect of their lives does not seem to have attracted the
attention it deserves, nor have the villas themselves, most of which
have disappeared. As the words 'pleasure-house' and 'play-house'
suggest, these villas were places for recreation as well as investments. Indeed, as we have seen, land was not an important investment for the elite in the latter part of the period, when references
to villas are most numerous. The names of some of the individual
houses confirm this impression that their use was for relaxation;
Willem Backer's* Buitensorg (Sans souci), Nicolaes Witsen's*
Tijdverdrijf (Pass the time) and Andries de Graeff's* Vredenhof
(Peace-haven) are among them.

The favourite sites for these villas were along the Amstel and
along the Vecht, from Muiden to Utrecht. This area was a bourgeois Arcadia, evoked in romances like the *Batavian Arcadia*
(1637), by Johan van Heemskerck, the brother-in-law of
Coenraed van Beuningen,* or the *Adriatic Rosamond* (1645) by
the German immigrant Philipp von Zesen, which describes a
Venetian nobleman living with his daughters in a villa on the
Amstel.[47] The appearance of the villas can be reconstructed from
the engravings by Daniel Stopendaal in *The Triumphant Vecht*,
published in 1719, a book which closely resembles Coronelli's
illustrations of Venetian villas ten years earlier. Other villas could
be found in Kennemerland, and a good number in 's Graveland,
including Andries Bicker's* Spanderswoud and Jan Six's* Jagtlust.
The growing importance of *villeggiatura* in the life of the Amsterdam elite may be gauged from the fact that at the end of the
seventeenth century the volumes of Resolutions of the Town
Council show that they were meeting relatively rarely, if at all, in
June and August. It is likely that its members had disappeared to
their pleasure-houses. It should be emphasized that what these
houses offered, like Venetian villas, was a temporary escape, and
not a permanent alternative to urban life. In this respect they
resemble their democratic equivalents for the Amsterdammers of
today, the chalets and allotments at Sloterdijk.

[47] Scholte (1916).

6

Training

This chapter is concerned with education, not in the relatively narrow sense of the formal training offered by schools and universities, though this of course is included, but in the wider sense of 'socialization', the whole process by which an older generation passes on its culture to a younger, starting from birth.

All too little is known about the early years of noble Venetians, in particular, and the remarks which follow are necessarily impressionistic and even speculative. However, the subject is too important to leave out. We have seen that the aristocratic household in Venice was often a large one, including not only brothers and sisters but also uncles and many servants. The father might be absent because he was serving as a naval officer, an ambassador or a *rettore* on the mainland. This is the situation, for example, underlying a letter written in 1540 by a noble Venetian lady to her husband, absent in Cyprus, giving him news of their five children: 'Lunardo is learning very well and I believe that we can expect well of him . . . Antonio . . . is beginning to speak and is my solace.' This passage is one of many documents from Renaissance Italy which could be cited against the famous thesis of the French historian Philippe Ariès to the effect that adults were not interested in childhood before the seventeenth century. 'Lunardo', then aged four, was the famous Doge Lunardo Donà* whose name has often occurred in these pages.[1]

---

[1] Seneca (1959), 9; Ariès (1960).

Mention has already been made of Zuan Dolfin, who left the church to look after his younger brothers when his father was employed away from Venice. The Venetian nobleman would be brought up not only by his mother and father (when his father was in town) but also by his uncles, his older siblings and the servants. There are reasons for surmising that he would be given to a wet-nurse (not suckled by his mother) and that he would be weaned late (by modern standards), at about the age of two. A famous treatise on family life was written by a fifteenth-century Venetian patrician, Francesco Barbaro, and it was still being reprinted in the sixteenth and seventeenth centuries. Barbaro makes the conventional suggestion that mothers suckle their children themselves, but goes on to give advice on the choice of a wet-nurse. The same points were made in 1633 by Antonino Colluraffi in advice directed specifically to Venetian nobles.[2] As for weaning, a physician whose book on the illnesses of children was published in Brescia, in Venetian territory, in 1577 warns parents that weaning after the age of two risks turning children into 'late developers' (*tardiusculi*). The need for this warning suggests that late weaning was a common practice.[3]

The Venetian nobleman was aware of social hierarchy right from the start because the household in which he grew up was a miniature version of the state in this respect. Servants, women and younger brothers were all supposed to know their places. It is likely that the child's emotional 'investment', as it has been called, was in the household and family as a whole rather than his parents alone. His training was likely to be strict, especially early in the period. The traditional form of training, as described by Barbaro, was to eat and drink little, to keep silent and to avoid 'excessive laughter'. This style of training in self-control certainly corresponds to the behaviour of well-known adult patricians at the beginning of the seventeenth century.

In the course of the century, however, changes in the training of noble children seem to have taken place. One late-seventeenth-century observer, a French Benedictine, noted the 'liberty' with

[2] Barbaro (1513); Colluraffi (1623–33), vol. 2, ch. 8.
[3] Ferrarius (1577).

which the children of nobles were then brought up.[4] Another
Frenchman commented that in patrician households fathers,
mothers and servants all idolized the children, who therefore grew
up proud, violent and accustomed to having their own way.[5]

Throughout the period noble children would seem to have been
given a warm, secure upbringing which would tend to discourage
them from leaving the family palace. An extended family is likely
to discourage the desire for achievement, since the individual is
never thrown on his own resources. The mechanism is likely to be
the more effective when the family is a noble one, for a nobleman's
sense of identity depended on his 'house' rather than on his own
achievements.

As for formal education, it was remarked by a foreign visitor
that in Venice 'the higher nobility . . . usually have their children
educated at home by private tutors'.[6] Silvestro Valier* and Zuan II
Corner* are known to have followed this pattern. Education
outside the home was dominated by the religious orders, with the
significant exception of the most famous teaching order of the
period, the Jesuits, who were objects of suspicion to many patricians (below, p. 104). Noble girls might be sent to convents. Noble
boys might be taught by the Dominicans, as in the case of Battista
Nani,* or by the Somaschi, as in that of Francesco da Molin.*
Boys might be sent to study outside Venice. Francesco Morosini*
was sent to the seminary of San Carlo at Modena, a training which
did not prevent him from making the most successful naval career
of the century.

At the age of about sixteen the young man might go on
to university (one girl did too, the famous bluestocking
Elena Lucrezia Corner, the illegitimate daughter of Zuanbattista
Corner*). University meant Padua – Venetians were forbidden
to study elsewhere (although Lunardo Donà* studied briefly at
Bologna in 1555).[7] How many of the elite went to Padua it is
unfortunately impossible to say, but at least eight out of the
twenty-five doges of the period did so. This proportion, about 30
per cent, may be typical of the upper nobility from whom the

---

4   Freschot (1709), 261.
5   Saint-Didier (1680), 302.
6   Freschot (1709), 261.
7   Seneca (1959), 9.

doges and proctors were usually drawn, in contrast to the lower nobility, who were ill educated and – if contemporary comment can be trusted – near illiterate. The point was that studying at Padua was expensive. Nicolò Contarini,* whose branch of that famous clan was not rich, may be described as having worked his way through university. He was a *camerlengo*, a minor Venetian official, in Padua when he was twenty.[8]

The most popular subjects of study at Padua were rhetoric, philosophy and law. Philosophy meant scholastic philosophy; the local Paduan brand of Aristotelianism was still strong in the seventeenth century. Between 1591 and 1631 the celebrated Cesare Cremonini taught at the university. His salary was double that of his colleague Galileo, and the Venetian Senate described him as 'the honour of Padua university', although he was three times investigated by the inquisition for alleged unorthodoxy – for a secret seminar on the mortality of the soul, for a joke at the expense of the devout who went to kiss the tomb of St Anthony at Padua and for his view that God was remote from the working of the universe. Cremonini was in a position to influence young men who would later be prominent in Venetian life, and the attitudes of Zuanfrancesco Loredan and his circle may owe something to his example.[9]

The informal education of patricians was no less important. Whether or not they could read or write, Venetian nobles learned what an anonymous Italian unkindly described as 'a certain style and a soft way of speaking accompanied by a grave manner which takes people in with ease'.[10] No more than in Oxford or Cambridge in the seventeenth century did the young gentlemen at Padua give their attention exclusively to the academic curriculum. Riding-schools, fencing-schools and dancing-schools were to be found there from the very beginning of the period.

In the seventeenth century travel was widely regarded as a form of education, political education in particular. Young men were supposed to observe not only the antiquities of the countries they visited but also their customs and laws. Travel was recommended

[8] Cozzi (1958), 55.
[9] Mabilleau (1881).
[10] Relatione 2, fo. 145r.

to Venetian noblemen precisely for this reason.[11] At least some
Venetian fathers followed this advice. For instance, Domenico
Contarini* and his brother Anzolo Contarini,* one a doge and the
other a well-known diplomat, were sent abroad when young to
gain experience of the courts of princes, 'so that' (as Domenico
explained in his will) 'we would be fit and able to govern the
commonwealth well'. In similar fashion Francesco Contarini*
travelled in France, Spain and Portugal, and Ferigo Corner* in
France, Spain and Germany. It was not uncommon for young men
of good families to travel in the suite of an ambassador. Giacomo
Foscarini* visited France in this way, and Pietro Basadonna*
visited Istanbul.

Another form of 'political novitiate', as one contemporary
called it, was institutionalized.[12] Patricians might be appointed
savio agl'ordini at about the age of twenty-five, essentially to learn
about affairs by listening to the discussions of the College. There
were five of these savi at a time, and they held office for six months
each. Lunardo Donà,* Agostino Nani* and Bertucci Valier* were
appointed savi at the age of twenty-five, Marcantonio Barbaro* at
twenty-three and Nicolò da Ponte* at about twenty-two.

The naval equivalent of this political novitiate was service at sea
as nobile di galera, a kind of midshipman learning how to command. Two posts were reserved for young nobles (sometimes only
twelve years old) on each galley, and six on each galleass. The
naval careers of Zuan Bembo* and Francesco Morosini,* among
others, started in this way.[13] These forms of service enabled well-
connected young men to overtake their contemporaries in the race
for office. Access to special training is of course one of the main
ways for an aristocracy to remain in power over the generations.

In Amsterdam as in Venice we know next to nothing about the all-
important early years of training, but the few scraps of information available suggest a considerable contrast between the two
cities. In Amsterdam the child of a member of the elite would be
brought up in a small household without uncles and without many

[11] Colluraffi (1623–33), vol. 1, ch. 9.
[12] Lupis (1663), 14.
[13] M. Nani Mocenigo (1935), 24.

servants. The household would be a more democratic society than was the case in Venice. The position of Dutch wives and servants was a favourable one which tended to surprise foreign visitors like the Frenchman Jean de Parival.[14]

It is reasonable to suspect less use of the wet-nurse in Amsterdam than in Venice, because servants were fewer, and earlier weaning, because there was less use of the wet-nurse. Melanie Klein has suggested that early weaning leads to anxiety in the infant, anxiety to greed, greed to ambition in the adult and ambition to achievement.[15] Whether this is generally the case or not, the Amsterdam elite were achievers, and they were criticized for greed more often than the Venetians. One might add that in their smaller households each individual would feel more need to achieve than the Venetians simply to survive economically; and that since they were commoners, their identity depended more on their achievements than the identity of noble Venetians did.

Education was probably even stricter in Amsterdam than in Venice. Calvinists tended to see little children as wicked, an idea associated with their stress on original sin. Dutch Calvinist parents, like New England Calvinist parents, believed in bringing up children in the 'fear of the Lord'.[16] The Dutch poet Jacob Cats, himself a member of the regent class, in Zeeland, stresses this feature of education in his *Marriage* (1624), a book which was widely read in the Dutch Republic in the seventeenth century. In the case of Amsterdam, his recommendations are confirmed by two leading members of the elite in his time, Pieter Schaep* (below, p. 109) and Willem Backer.*[17]

Body shame seems to have been more acute in Dutch society than elsewhere in Europe. Nicolaes Witsen,* on a visit to Russia, recorded his shock at seeing men and women bathing naked, 'like animals, without shame'.[18] The extraordinary cleanliness of Dutch houses, at least in towns, made an indelible impression on visitors from England and France, especially the need to take off one's

---

[14] Parival (1661), 20, 25. Cf. Murris (1925) and Schama (1987), 407–12.
[15] M. Klein (1960).
[16] Morgan (1944), ch. 3.
[17] GA, Bicker papers, no. 717; GA, Backer papers, no. 66.
[18] Witsen (1966–7), vol. 1, 441.

shoes on entering and to refrain from spitting, at least on the floor.[19] It is therefore likely that the virtues of cleanliness and order were instilled into Amsterdam patrician children at an early age, and helped form adults who were, by the standards of seventeenth-century Europe, unusually well disciplined. In short, it is tempting to compare the childhood of the Amsterdammers with that of the Yurok Indians as brilliantly described by the psychoanalyst Erik Erikson. However different the two social cultures were in other respects, we find the same stress on both thrift and cleanliness. The Yurok were a society of salmon fishers, and the wealth of Amsterdam too was originally founded on fish – on the trade in herring.[20]

The beginning of our period, 1578, is a significant date in the history of Amsterdam education for negative reasons. The monastic schools were abolished, leaving only private schools and the 'public gymnasia', or grammar schools, on the Old Side and the New Side of Amsterdam. The one on the Old Side was the more famous; in the early seventeenth century the best-known teacher was a Devonshire man, Matthew Slade, at one time a Brownist. The Town Council took a considerable interest in the school, appointing 'scholarchs' from its own members to govern it, among them Gerard Schaep,* Nicolaes Tulp,* Jacob de Graeff* and Cornelis de Graeff.* Some of the elite certainly studied there: Willem Backer,* for example, Nicolaes Tulp,* Nicolaes Witsen* and Coenraed van Beuningen.* Lists of pupils survive from 1685 onwards, which show that the school then contained about two hundred pupils with a good many patrician names among them. Competition between the pupils was encouraged by the award of prizes. Thus in 1704 Joannes Corver, who came from the famous family of burgomasters, received the prize for diligence, with a special report on his ability and his spurring on the other pupils.[21] Yet another clue to the importance of individual achievement in Amsterdam culture.

Some idea of the proficiency in Latin and of the values instilled at the school emerges from the verses recited publicly by a star

[19] Parival (1661), 25; Temple (1673), 96. Cf. Zumthor (1959), 138, and Schama (1987), 387–4.
[20] Erikson (1950), ch. 4.
[21] GA, Curatoren van de openbare gymnasia, no. 19.

pupil at the beginning of the academic year and published after-
wards, for example the encomium on the VOC delivered by Jan
Backer*, then aged sixteen, or the 'metrical oration' on the need
for civic harmony delivered by Jan Trip* in 1681.[22] It was also
possible to learn 'a little Greek' there, as Nicolaes Witsen* records
in his autobiography.[23] All this evidence refers to the later part of
the period. The earlier period is much more obscure; although we
know from his papers that C. P. Hooft* (born in 1547) was able
to quote Livy freely in Latin, we do not know whether he was
exceptional or typical of his generation.

From school, over a third of the Amsterdam elite went on to
university, the most obvious choice being Leiden, which had been
founded in 1575. Over fifty members of the group studied there.[24]
There was no compulsion to go to one particular university. At
least eight members of the elite studied at Franeker University in
Friesland.[25] Others were sent abroad: Martin Coster* studied at
Ferrara, Pieter Schaep* at Heidelberg, Gerard Schaep* at Orléans,
Volckert Overlander* at Basel, Andries de Graeff* at Poitiers and
François de Vicq* at Padua. Among the subjects of study, the most
popular choice (on the part of the fathers, if not necessarily the
sons) was the law. At Leiden thirty of the elite matriculated in law,
compared with ten in philosophy, eight in 'letters' and one (Frans
Reael* in 1637) in history, an unusual choice at the time, though
history lectures there were given by scholars of high calibre such as
Lipsius, Merula and Heinsius.

From 1632 onwards there was an institution of higher education at Amsterdam itself: the Athenaeum.[26] It seems to have been
used as a stage between school and university; indeed, in the late
seventeenth century the top class at the Latin school might pass
straight on to the Athenaeum. What made the Athenaeum especially important was its curriculum – a new foundation can more
easily teach new subjects and drop old ones than a traditional
institution can. The Athenaeum was inaugurated with a lecture by
Caspar Barlaeus on philosophy and one by Gerard Vossius on

[22] Backer (1678); Trip (1681).
[23] Witsen (1872), 41.
[24] Rieu (1875).
[25] Fockema Andreae and Meijer (1968).
[26] Dibon (1954), 220ff.

history. Both men were Arminians (Barlaeus had lost his teaching post at Leiden for this reason), which shows which faction was in the ascendancy at Amsterdam in 1632. The inaugural lectures of both professors suggest a pragmatic approach to their respective subjects: Barlaeus spoke on 'the wise merchant' (*mercator sapiens*), and Vossius on 'the use of history'.[27]

The natural sciences soon became an important part of the curriculum at the Athenaeum. In the middle of the seventeenth century mathematics, astronomy, botany and medicine were all being taught there. Some of the teachers were sympathetic to Descartes and his philosophy at a time when he was considered a dangerous innovator elsewhere, in Leiden as in France. Professor de Raey, for instance, who taught at the Athenaeum from 1669, tried to make a synthesis of Aristotle and Descartes, and later the supporters of Descartes seem to have triumphed, since an edition of the works of Descartes was published in 1694 for the use of the Athenaeum students. An interest in history and the natural sciences, sympathy for intellectual innovation and a Cartesian cast of mind were all encouraged, if not implanted, by the teachers at the Athenaeum.

There was one political institution in Amsterdam with a function not unlike the post of *savio agl'ordini* at Venice. This was the 'secretary', a junior appointment often held by young men of patrician family, sometimes years before they themselves entered the Town Council. Thus Coenraed van Beuningen* became secretary when he was twenty-one, and entered the Council when he was thirty-eight; Gerrit Hooft* became secretary when he was twenty-four, and entered the Council at thirty; Cornelis Munter* became secretary at twenty-four and councillor at forty-nine.

Travel was an important kind of informal education in Amsterdam as in Venice. In the early years of the period it might be undertaken for business reasons – C. P. Hooft* travelled 'eastwards', as he put it, probably to Königsberg, spending three or four years there when he was an apprentice merchant (*iong coopgesel*) in his early twenties. In other cases the travel was more politically oriented. Coenraed van Beuningen* went to Paris in 1642, at the age of twenty, as a secretary to the celebrated Grotius,

[27] Barlaeus (1632); Vossius (1632); Dibon (1954), 225ff.

while Nicolaes Witsen* went to Moscow in 1664, aged twenty-three, in the suite of the ambassador, Jacob Boreel.*

Other patricians made the Grand Tour (groote tour, speelreis), with or without a tutor.[28] In 1591, for example, the famous scholar Lipsius went abroad as tutor to seven young Netherlanders, including the twenty-year-old Jacob de Graeff.* Jacob's son Cornelis de Graeff* went to Paris in his twenties. Joan Huydecoper* the younger went to France and Italy. On his return from Russia Nicolaes Witsen* visited (among other places) Paris, Milan, Florence, Rome, Geneva and Frankfurt.

It is likely that both the Venetians and the Amsterdammers were, for economic as well as political reasons, more widely travelled than most governing elites in seventeenth-century Europe, in spite of the growing international fashion for the Grand Tour. Early travel might be regarded as socialization into tolerance, which would help to explain the remarkable stress on that value among both patriciates. The attitudes and values of the two elites are the subject of the following chapter.

---

[28] Frank-van Westrienen (1983).

7

Attitudes and Values

Compared with the other noblemen of seventeenth-century Europe, the Venetians had another peculiarity which has not yet been mentioned: they liked writing books. Thanks to the useful compilation of P. A. Zeno, we know that the Venetian nobility as a whole published more than a hundred books between 1580 and 1658; the most popular categories were poems, plays, orations, philosophy and history, in that order.[1] The books published by members of the elite include Nicolò da Ponte's* treatise on geometry, said to have been published in the year of his death, 1585; Nicolò Contarini's* *The Perfection of the Universe* (1576), a general survey which makes him the one member of the group to offer an explicit world-view; Polo Paruta's* *Perfection of Political Life* (1579; his *Discourses* and his *History of Venice* were published after his death); Battista Nani's* *History of Venice* (1662); Zuan Sagredo's* romance, *Arcadia on the Brenta*, written when he was young and published in 1655 under an anagrammatic pseudonym, and his *History of the Ottoman Empire* (1673), written when he was mature and published under his own name.

The unpublished treatises by members of the elite form an almost equally important collection. They include the poems of Simone Contarini* and of Antonio Ottobon,* the latter in dialect;

---

[1] Zeno (1662).

Daniele IV Dolfin's* treatise on the art of war; Polo Tiepolo's* history of Cyprus; and, most famous of all, Nicolò Contarini's* history of Venice, which had a considerable circulation in manuscript. This last book remained unpublished for political reasons. A working party advised the Council of Ten that the book contained maxims of state which were better kept secret than divulged.[2]

The fact that the other treatises were not published suggests the Venetian emphasis on the role of the cultivated amateur. Seventeenth-century European nobles who published books often liked to protest that they were not professional writers (still a low-status group in this period), but in Venice the ideal of the amateur seems even more important than elsewhere. As we have seen, it even affected their political system. This amateur ideal is expressed most explicitly in Antonino Colluraffi's *The Venetian Noble* (1623–33), a treatise on the education of the nobility by a professional tutor, but it is supported by other testimonies. One Venetian nobleman who dabbled in literature (Z. F. Sagredo, brother of Zaccaria Sagredo*) once declared, 'I am a Venetian gentleman and I have never hoped to be known as a literary man.' One suspects irony behind that 'hoped'.[3] Zuan Sagredo* described the noble heroes of his *Arcadia on the Brenta* as 'well informed but not academic, carrying their learning lightly' (*dotti senza professione, eruditi senza ostentatione*).[4] Zuanfrancesco Loredan, sometime councillor of Ten and the leading literary figure of mid-century Venice, was said to devote his days to politics and to write his stories only at night.[5]

Again, Battista Nani's* history of Venice gave one contemporary the impression that it had been written in haste by a man preoccupied with other matters. Nani* was in fact an extremely active diplomat, who was elected ambassador seven times. Perhaps the unpolished impression given by his history was a deliberate one, an example of what the Renaissance nobleman Baldassare Castiglione called *sprezzatura*, in other words the

[2] Cozzi (1958), 200n; N. Contarini (1982).
[3] Bouwsma (1968), 87.
[4] Sagredo (1655), 1.
[5] Lupis (1663), 25.

deliberate attempt to give the impression of effortlessness. Nani*
was famous for having the ear of the house: 'When he speaks in
the Senate, the whole place is hushed.'⁶ But the Senate did not like
polish; it preferred 'Attic' prose to 'Asiatic', a plain or 'senatorial'
speech to an ornate or 'academic' one.⁷

In short, the Venetians tended to have a pragmatic cast of mind
and to prefer figures of arithmetic – as Sir Robert Walpole once
remarked of the House of Commons – to figures of rhetoric. This
tendency can be documented from the *relazioni*, the reports which
returning diplomats and administrators of the mainland had to
read out in public. They are cool in tone and full of precise facts
and figures. These reports are also good evidence of Venetian
concern for history, since they regularly explain the situation in
France, say, or in the Ottoman Empire by making reference to the
past. Another sign of the elite's historical-mindedness is the fact
that the Venetian government regularly appointed official historians. The histories of Paruta,* Contarini* and Nani* were all
commissioned in this way.⁸ This interest in history was pragmatic.
History should be written, Nicolò Contarini* remarked, not to
exhibit eloquence but to help in political affairs. The historian
could render this assistance, so it was often thought in the seventeenth century, by formulating political maxims and illustrating
them with examples, so that readers could extract political observations for meditation, as Lunardo Donà* did when he was
reading Guicciardini's *History of Italy*.⁹

Venetian official history was of course, among other things, an
instrument of propaganda, the literary equivalent of the historical
paintings in the Doge's Palace. But interest in the past was not
entirely utilitarian. The library of Ferigo Contarini* included
forty-five books on Roman antiquities, on coins, medals, inscriptions, statues, triumphs, families, religion and military discipline.¹⁰
Venetian nobles liked to identify themselves with Romans. They
had a predilection for such classical terms as 'senate', 'toga' or

⁶   EIP, 34.
⁷   Croll (1921).
⁸   Cozzi (1963–4).
⁹   Seneca (1959), 36.
¹⁰ Cipollato (1961).

'patrician'. The Corner clan – and the Venetian clan was not so unlike the Roman *gens* – claimed descent from the Roman Cornelii, the Loredan from Mutius Scaevola and the Zustinian from the Emperor Justinian.[11]

There is much less evidence of patrician interest in the natural sciences ('natural philosophy' was the term used at the time), although such an interest did exist. The best-known example is that of Zuanfrancesco Sagredo, not himself a member of the elite but a close relative of some of them. He was friendly with Galileo, who made Sagredo a character in two of his dialogues. He was interested in astronomy and magnetism, had his own workshop and even made scientific instruments.[12] Another important example is Nicolò Contarini,* whose *The Perfection of the Universe* discusses the elements and the planets (besides God and the angels). Contarini* encouraged the medical researches of Dr Santorio Santorio, was interested in hydraulics and had 'a large machine' constructed in his garden to raise water.[13] Both he and Lunardo Donà* were regular visitors to the Accademia Cacciatrice, where discussions on the natural sciences took place (above, p. 81), and Donà* was friendly with Galileo.[14] Battista Nani* and other members of his academy, the Filaleti (Truthlovers), were interested in botany, while Zuanbattista Corner* owned 'mathematical and geometrical instruments'.[15] Polo Antonio Belegno* and Anzolo Diedo* were interested in machines. Belegno* had 'a hydraulic machine' constructed to serve his palace and its garden.

These examples must not be given too much emphasis. The Cacciatrice was equally concerned with questions of theology and ethics, and in general it may be argued that the Venetian ethos of the aristocratic amateur was a discouragement to scientific research. It allowed only two attitudes to the natural sciences. The first was a collector's interest. Ferigo Contarini* had a typically eclectic cabinet of curiosities of the years around 1600 which

[11]   Chambers (1970), 12ff.
[12]   Favaro (1902).
[13]   Cozzi (1958), 57; Tenenti (1959); Favaro (1883), vol. 2, 74.
[14]   Favaro (1883), vol. 2, 94.
[15]   Romanin (1853–61), vol. 7, 557; Sansovino (1663), 371.

included minerals and bones, a cat's testicles and a buffalo's horn.[16] The second possible attitude to the natural sciences was the utilitarian attitude of a governing elite. When Galileo was a professor at Padua, Antonio Priuli* and Zaccaria Sagredo,* together with other patricians and accompanied by Galileo himself, ascended the campanile of Piazza San Marco 'to see the marvels and singular effects of the telescope of the said Galileo'. A rise in the professor's salary followed immediately. Of course a telescope had practical value for a naval power.[17]

This pragmatic or utilitarian approach is summed up in Colluraffi's treatise on education, which recommends the Venetian noble student to leave 'subtle and over-curious investigations' to others, and to study mathematics only in so far as it is relevant to 'the interests of the commonwealth'.[18] Mathematics was associated with military studies in a Paduan academy for Venetian nobles, the Delia, founded by Pietro Duodo when he was *capitano* of Padua in 1607, believing as he did that the 'mathematical sciences' were necessary knowledge for 'a perfect gentleman and soldier' (*perfetto cavaliere e soldato*). The Delia later on had Zuan Pesaro* as its 'protector'.[19]

This brief sketch of the interest of Venetian nobles confirms William Bouwsma's emphasis on the pragmatic, empirical nature of the Venetian style of thought.[20] But it would not do to forget that it was also deeply marked by scholasticism, especially the local variety, the Aristotelianism of the 'school of Padua'. Nicolò Contarini's* book on the perfection of the universe discusses the opinions of Aquinas, Ockham and Gregory of Rimini. Lunardo Donà* was particularly interested in the philosophy of Aquinas. Descartes, on the other hand, seems to have made little impact on seventeenth-century Venice, though his ideas and those of Malebranche are discussed by the philosopher Bernardo Trevisan in his *Philosophical Meditations* (1704). In 1600 Venetians had been abreast of new ideas, but in 1700 this was no longer the case. Tradition was powerful and the propensity to innovate was weak.

[16]   Cipollato (1961). Cf. Impey and Macgregor (1985), Pomian (1987).
[17]   Favaro (1891), 69.
[18]   Colluraffi (1623–33), vol. 1, 56.
[19]   Favaro (1883), vol. 2, 2, and document xci.
[20]   Bouwsma (1968).

Perhaps this was the price of their notable past achievements. However, this conservatism may – as Addison thought – have contributed to Venetian economic decline, for 'a trading nation must be still for new changes, and expedients as different junctures and emergencies arise'.[21]

The Amsterdam elite also published books, but they give a rather different impression. Their publications include a book on magnetism by Laurens Reael;* the observations on medicine of Nicolaes Tulp;* the treatises on botany of Joan Commelin;* the atlases of the publisher Joan Blaeu;* a tragedy, Medea, by Jan Six;* the religious outpourings of Coenraed van Beuningen;* Joannes Hudde's* letters on algebra and geometry; and, best known of all, two books by Nicolaes Witsen,* one on shipbuilding and one on north and east Tartary. This list, which makes no claim to be exhaustive, suggests a much greater interest in the natural sciences than there was in Venice. One might add the fact that two of the elite, P. J. Hooft* and Jacob de Graeff,* shared a laboratory and were supposed to have discovered the secret of perpetual motion. P. J. Hooft* also studied medicine and chemistry.

The list suggests that the Amsterdam patricians took rather less interest in history than the Venetians, but this point needs qualification. Amsterdam, like Venice, had an official historian at one point, the Lombard Gregorio Leti, appointed in 1689.[22] One of the most distinguished historians in seventeenth-century Europe, P. C. Hooft, 'the Dutch Tacitus', was the son of a burgomaster of Amsterdam, C. P. Hooft,* who was not ignorant of history either. C. P. Hooft's* papers refer to sixteen historical works which include Livy, Josephus, Guicciardini, Sleidan (who wrote on sixteenth-century German political and ecclesiastical affairs), Foxe, Camden (the Annals) and the Dutch historian Pieter Bor.[23]

The books belonging to burgomaster Martin Coster* testify to his historical learning. He owned copies of Herodotus, Thucydides, Xenophon, Livy, Plutarch and Josephus, to mention

---

[21]   Addison (1705), 84.
[22]   Cameroni (1893).
[23]   H. A. E. van Gelder (1918), Appendix 2.

only ancient historians. Among the moderns, his library included the antiquarian studies of the Italian humanist Flavio Biondo, the chronicle of the German Sebastian Franck, the memoirs of Philippe de Commynes and the history of his own time by the Italian bishop Paolo Giovio. He also owned the history of France by Paolo Emilio, the history of Poland by Martin Cromer, the history of England by Polidore Vergil and the history of Florence by Machiavelli. If there was any 'Renaissance man' among the Amsterdam elite, it was surely Coster,* who had in fact studied in Italy in the mid sixteenth century.[24] However, there was another virtuoso among the aldermen and burgomasters a century later. Nicolaes Witsen* was an enthusiastic antiquarian. He was fascinated by the diversity of languages and customs, as well as being interested in the design of triremes, in the ships represented in Egyptian hieroglyphics and on medieval seals, in an ancient mirror found in Siberia and in the authenticity of a so-called Roman shield discovered by the English scholar Dr John Woodward.[25]

This interest in history was in part a utilitarian one. P. C. Hooft, dedicating his biography of Henri IV of France to Dirck Bas,* discussed the special value of history to rulers. C. P. Hooft* regularly argued from historical precedent in the Town Council. He quoted the fact that Moses was above Aaron as an 'example' which proved that the preachers of Amsterdam should not tell the Council what to do.[26] As in Venice, the patricians of Amsterdam looked back to antiquity for inspiration. The Dutch preoccupation with the revolt of their ancestors the Batavians against Rome is well known. It was expressed in P. C. Hooft's play *Baeto* (1626) and Vondel's play *The Batavian Brothers* (1662), as well as in paintings by Rembrandt and Govert Flinck for the Amsterdam Town Hall (below, p. ••). In these cases the Dutch identified themselves with their ancestors the Batavians and the Spanish empire with that of Rome.[27]

However, the Dutch could not resist seeing themselves as new Romans, at least on occasion. In a pamphlet called *Fin de la*

---

[24] GA, Weeskamer, Boedelpapieren, Lade 139.
[25] Gebhard (1881); Rietbergen (1986); Levine (1977), 173–4.
[26] C. P. Hooft (1871–1925), vol. 1, 97.
[27] Waal (1952); Schöffer (1975); Schama (1987), 76–81.

guerre, for instance, published in Amsterdam in the early seventeenth century, Scipio Africanus and Fabius Maximus talk about the best way to attack Carthage, and the dialogue slides into the argument that Spain should be attacked in her most vulnerable spot, the West Indies.[28] The books and funeral monuments of members of the Amsterdam elite often carry Latin inscriptions referring to them as *consul* (if burgomaster) or *senator* (if a member of the Town Council). Alternatively, like the inscriptions to some paintings in the Town Hall, they might refer to Scipio or Fabius Maximus as 'burgomasters' of Rome.

The Amsterdam elite, as one might have expected from a largely Calvinist group, also identified with Old Testament figures such as Solomon and Moses, just as the Dutch Protestants identified themselves with the children of Israel as a chosen people – and Philip of Spain with Pharaoh. In the Town Hall the councillor's chamber contained one painting of Solomon praying for wisdom and one of Moses advised by Jethro; the magistrate's chamber contained a painting of Moses and the Tables of the Law.[29]

The idea that history is a storehouse of political examples was of course common enough in seventeenth-century Europe. What is much less common is to find a ruling group so interested in the natural sciences. One obvious reason for this interest was the presence of professional doctors on the Town Council, something without an equivalent in Venice. Nicolaes Tulp's* scientific learning sprang from his medical studies. Another reason for interest in the natural sciences was something shared with Venice, the involvement of the elite with the sea. This may explain why Admiral Dr Laurens Reael* should have written on magnetism, and why Willem Blaeu*, sometime pupil of the great Danish astronomer Tycho Brahe, should have decided to come to Amsterdam to make globes and maps, passing on his geographical interests to his son Joan Blaeu.*

In the case of Nicolaes Witsen,* on the other hand, disinterested intellectual curiosity seems to have been predominant, in his scientific studies as in his historical ones. Witsen* was interested in mammoths and in comets and in the question of whether a

[28] K.3428.
[29] Fremantle (1959); Groenhuis (1981); Schama (1987), ch. 2.

so-called unicorn's horn really belonged to a narwhal. He was a
fellow of the Royal Society of London, and corresponded with its
members about unusual shells and the question of whether Nova
Zembla was a continent.[30] Disinterested curiosity also seems to
have been predominant in Joannes Hudde,* who was said to be
one of the best mathematicians of his day, was interested in
astronomy, optics and medicine and was on friendly terms with
Huygens, Leibniz and Spinoza. Hudde* abandoned his studies for
a political career, but retained an interest in hydraulics and was in
charge of the technical side of operations when the dykes were
broken in 1672 as a last defence against the French invaders.[31] It
may be suspected, however, that the social background of Witsen*
and Hudde* was relevant to their interests. In his book on shipbuilding Witsen* betrayed a fascination with technical details,
such as the exact measurements of planks, which in other parts of
Europe might have been thought beneath a gentleman. He even
drew some of the illustrations himself, just as he had once made
etchings to illustrate Ovid's *Metamorphoses*. Again, Hudde* had
no inhibitions about the pursuit of such 'subtle and over-curious
investigations' as mathematics. Perhaps Witsen* and Hudde*
were able to indulge their interests because they did not identify
with noble values.

Novelty, that entrepreneurial virtue, seems to have been accepted more easily in seventeenth-century Amsterdam than in
Venice, or indeed most parts of Europe in the period. As C. P.
Hooft* put it, 'not all novelty is bad and not all antiquity is good'.
His defence of novelty was to quote instances of valuable new
discoveries in astronomy, medicine and navigation; an interest in
innovation and an interest in the natural sciences went naturally
together.[32] An interest in novelty was also expressed in two inaugural lectures at the Amsterdam Athenaeum, where a number of
the elite were educated, as we have seen. Professor Blasius lectured
in 1659 on 'New Discoveries', discussing Harvey and the circulation of the blood, while Professor de Raey lectured in 1669 on

---

[30] Gebhard (1881), esp. vol. 2.
[31] *NNBW*, vol. 1, cols 1172–6.
[32] C. P. Hooft (1871–1925), vol. 1, 206.

Piáceri, che prendono i Nobeli di Venetia nel tempo dell'in uernata nell'uccellare nelle lagune
in torno alla Città nelle loro fisolere, et altre sorte di barchette con archi da balle et
schioppi, taluolta accompagnati alcuni di essi; dalle loro Signore
franco forma con priuilegio

1 The patricians at play: nobles fowling on the Venetian lagoons, armed with guns and *archi da balle* – bows loaded with terracotta pellets.

2 Amsterdam informality: B. van de Helst's portrait of Daniel Bernard* (1626–1714), for twenty-seven years a member of the Town Council. There are East India Company documents on the table.

Chiesa del Reden̄tore di Capuzini

Franco Ferma con Priuilegio

I Procuratori di S. Marcho, così detti dalla cura et amministratione che hanno dell'entrate di quell'augustiss.º Tempio uestono perpetuamente la toga, essendo q.ta dignità suᵖma nella Republica.

3 Venetian formality: proctor in official robes.

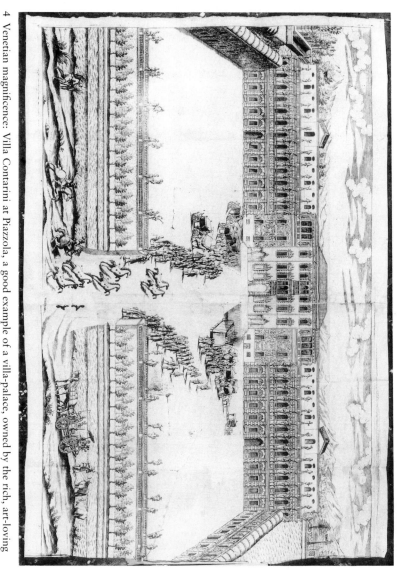

4 Venetian magnificence: Villa Contarini at Piazzola, a good example of a villa-palace, owned by the rich, art-loving Marco Contarini* (1631–89).

5 Amsterdam simplicity: Gunterstein on the Vecht, a villa owned by Ferdinand
van Collen* (1651–1735).

6 Church of San Moisè, Venice. A flamboyant piece
of baroque architecture and sculpture, commissioned
by Vincenzo Fini,* one of the few parvenus in the
Venetian elite.

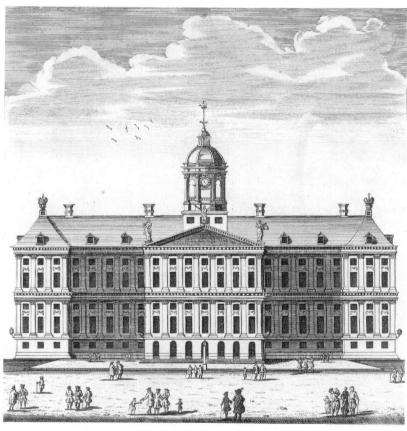

7 The Town Hall of Amsterdam. The monumental simplicity of the design reflects Dutch bourgeois taste. The baroque sculpture in the pediments is rendered unobtrusive in this print.

8 Willem van Loon* (1633–95) at the age of thirty months. He became burgomaster fifty years later.

9 Even babies who died in infancy were commemorated in art, not as individuals but as members of leading patrician families (in this case the de Graeffs).

'The Wisdom of the Ancients', suggesting that some ancient 'wisdom' was not wisdom at all.[33]

The style of thought of C. P. Hooft* has been characterized as empiricist, rationalist and individualist.[34] In the course of the seventeenth century, however, one can observe the penetration, in patrician circles, of a consciously mathematical style of thought which owes not a little to Descartes and to Spinoza. An example of the application of the geometrical method to political decision-making can be found among the papers of Joannes Hudde.* Hudde* is commenting on a project of defensive alliance with France. He begins with a definition of a 'defensive alliance', then states an axiom, that the chief aim of all individuals and states is their own conservation, and concludes that the idea of a defensive alliance with an enemy is absurd.[35]

These examples may tempt the historian to exaggerate the modernity of the Amsterdam elite, their combination of rationalism, Protestantism, capitalism and science. As a corrective, it might be valuable to look at the case of Coenraed van Beuningen.* Van Beuningen* is best known as a highly skilled diplomatic negotiator, but he was also a man of wide interests, including literature, history and the natural sciences. He was friendly with the biologist Jan Swammerdam, and interested in the ideas of Descartes. He combined all this with an interest in mysticism, millenarianism, astrology, dream interpretation and 'supernatural wonders'. Van Beuningen* may well have been a schizoid type. He suffered a breakdown in 1688, and went round the streets preaching about the end of the world; he was placed under guardianship. However, to dismiss his non-rational interests as nothing but a form of madness would be a superficial interpretation. Many sane people in the seventeenth century shared these interests. Van Beuningen* is a fascinating but not an isolated example of the coexistence of new science, Cartesianism, astrology and millenarianism inside one man's head.[36]

---

[33] Thijssen-Schoutte (1954), 246, 125ff.
[34] H. A. E. van Gelder (1918).
[35] GA, J. Hudde, Brieven en papieren, no. 49.
[36] Roldanus (1931).

The religious attitudes of the patricians of Venice and Amsterdam were more alike than one might have expected, given that one city was officially Catholic and the other predominantly Protestant. In Venice 'Catholic' and 'Papist' were not the same, observed the French ambassador Philippe Canaye de Fresnes even before the Interdict. After the Pope had laid Venice under interdict in 1606, following a serious clash of jurisdictions, the Venetian case was presented by the Republic's official theologian, Paolo Sarpi. In Sarpi's writings the difference between 'Catholic' and 'Papist' is clear enough. Sarpi believed that the primitive church (representing the true 'Catholic' position) had been democratic, poor, unworldly and austere, while the contemporary ('Papist') church was monarchical, rich, worldly and corrupt; that the great obstacle to the necessary reform of the church was the triple alliance of the Pope, Spain and the Jesuits; and that the Augustinian emphasis on man's need for grace was nearer the truth than the Jesuit emphasis on free will.[37]

Was Sarpi's view the view of the Venetian elite? A similar cluster of attitudes can certainly be found in Nicolò Contarini,* a man of austere morality who wanted the church to keep out of temporal affairs and hated the Jesuits for their use of religion as a political tool. Augustinian on the question of grace, he followed the Calvinist synod of Dort (Dordrecht) in the Netherlands, with interest, and his sympathies were not, as one might have expected, with the Arminians (sometimes accused of being Catholics in disguise) but with the Gomarists (below, p. 108). His was an interior religion, and his will makes an unusually brief mention of the Virgin and the saints.[38] Some of these attitudes can be found among other patricians of the period. Lunardo Donà,* for instance, was equally anti-Spanish and critical of the papacy, though he was not opposed to Counter-Reformation spirituality. He studied the devotional writings of San Carlo Borromeo and Fray Luis de Granada, noting that the latter should be 'read twice a year'.[39] Antonio Priuli,* according to his will, hoped to reach heaven 'thanks only to the blood shed for us by Our Lord Jesus Christ', a

[37]   On Sarpi, contrast Cozzi (1959b), Burke (1967) and Wootton (1983).
[38]   Cozzi (1958), 211ff.
[39]   Seneca (1959), 36.

truly remarkable formula coming from the lips of an apparently
Catholic nobleman. Nicolò da Ponte* was interested in St Augus-
tine, and defended the Venetian heretic Buccella; his brother
Andrea fled to Calvin's Geneva; Pope Pius V thought him a bad
Catholic, though the patriarch of Jerusalem thought him a good
one.[40]

The reports of some patricians who had served as ambassadors
to Rome show that they were anti-Spanish and hostile to the Pope
for supporting Spain. Examples which spring to mind are Polo
Tiepolo,* Polo Paruta,* Agostino Nani* and Simone Contarini.*
One might describe this group, which overlaps if it does not
coincide with the faction of the 'youngsters' in Venetian politics,
as anti-papal, in the sense of opposing the jurisdictional claims of
the Pope, and anti-clerical, at least in the sense of opposing clerical
exemption from lay justice and lay taxation. There is also some
evidence, from members of the nobility if not from members of the
elite, of more radical unorthodoxy. Zuanfrancesco Loredan and
his circle are the most famous examples of what the seventeenth
century called 'libertines' (associating free thought with free
love).[41]

It would be misleading, however, not to mention equally outstanding examples of an opposed religious attitude. On these
issues the elite were not cohesive. There was a devout party – or,
if 'party' is too strong a term, a faction or a group – of patricians
who were more favourably disposed towards the papacy. Papal
families were regularly made honorary Venetian nobles; the
Aldobrandini, the Peretti, even the Borghese, the family of Pope
Paul V, the pope who laid Venice under interdict. The more
prominent members of the devout faction included Zuanne
Dolfin,* who ended his life as a cardinal (it was said that he was
elected proctor as a reward for bringing some important relics to
Venice);[42] Marin Grimani,* who was knighted by Pope Sixtus V
and left money for masses to be said by the Jesuits; Zuan Pesaro,*
another supporter of the Jesuits; Ferigo Contarini,* described by
the nuncio at Venice in 1593 as 'always favourable to the church';

[40] Stella (1964), 13ff; Stella (1967), 132.
[41] Spini (1950).
[42] Cozzi (1958), 218.

and Giacomo Foscarini,* who wanted to have the Jesuit college at Padua reopened. Another leading member of the devout faction was Zuan I Corner,* described by the Spanish ambassador as 'fearful of God', whose son was a cardinal, and to whom was dedicated a treatise on Venetian relics written by the noble priest Zuan Tiepolo.[43]

If one examines the wills made by members of the elite over the whole period, it is to find, in the majority of cases, considerable emphasis on the outward forms of religion which make the testaments of Nicolò Contarini* and Antonio Priuli* seem exceptional. The proctors ask to be buried in the habit of a Franciscan or a Capuchin; they leave money for three hundred, five hundred or even three thousand masses (there was an inflation of masses in this period); they express their devotion to patron saints and – a relatively new cult – to guardian angels. Zuan Bembo* once offered a silver ship to the Holy House of Loreto; Zuan I Corner* asked for someone to make a pilgrimage there in his name; and Alvise Barbarigo* kept the relics of San Sulpicio in his villa.

Individual examples like this are of course a poor substitute for a questionnaire on the subject. The nearest equivalent we owe to the Jesuits, who made a survey in 1620 about the attitude of senators to the readmission of the society to Venice. They estimated that at least half the senators were opposed to them. The fact that Venice opposed the Pope up to the point of interdict and beyond in 1606 suggests that the majority of the ruling elite at this point supported an anti-papal policy in the sense that they saw the Pope as acting merely as a temporal prince when he attacked the 'liberties' or privileges of Venice. Yet the wills of the elite suggest that most of them accepted an exterior religion, an impression confirmed by such a collective act of devotion as the building of the Church of the *Salute* by order of the Senate as what the fabric committee called 'an appropriate means to placate the wrath of heaven', following the terrible plague of 1630.[44] How is one to reconcile the apparent contradiction? It looks as if what happened in 1606 was that at a time when Venice seemed threatened by Spain and the Pope was a friend of Spain, the silent majority of

---

[43] Tiepolo (1617).
[44] Moschini (1842), 27.

patricians were prepared to accept the leadership of a hardline anti-papal group whose other religious attitudes they did not share.

Curiously enough, this was exactly the situation in some Dutch towns during the revolt of the Netherlands. The fear of Spain persuaded the silent majority to accept the leadership of a minority of Calvinists. Thus in Amsterdam in 1578 a group of former religious exiles took over the city government. They included Wilhelm Baerdesen,* Reynier Cant* (a leading Calvinist who had been living in Bremen), Martin Coster,* Adriaen Cromhout* (another leading Calvinist who had been living in Medemblik), Dirck Graeff* (another Calvinist who had found it prudent to retire to Emden) and Adriaen Pauw* (who had been living in Emden and Hamburg). For some years it was still possible for Catholics to serve on the Amsterdam Town Council. An example is Ysbrant Dommer,* who joined in 1578 and remained there till his death in about 1582. Even when the Catholics disappeared from office, a group within the elite still stood up for religious toleration. The most famous member of this group was C. P. Hooft.* With his dislike of religious persecution, on the part of Catholics and Protestants alike, went a dislike of subtle theological disputations and of the ambition of the clergy and a conception of Christianity as a matter of 'good conscience' rather than a matter of deep theological questions. In short, Hooft* practised an 'interior religion' (the term innerlycke religieusheydt was his own). Like Sir Thomas Browne, Hooft* might have said, 'I condemn not all things in the Council of Trent' (he owned a book by the Counter-Reformation controversialist Cardinal Baronio) 'nor approve all in the synod of Dort', the Dutch synod which declared it incumbent on Calvinists to believe that all men are totally depraved and that God has elected only a few to salvation.[45]

C. P. Hooft* married a Blaeu, and it is unlikely that the Blaeu family were strong Calvinists either. At any rate Joan Blaeu* used to print missals (with 'Cologne' on the title-page) for export to the Catholic world. Perhaps this was no more significant than the trade with Spain which Andries Bicker,* for example, engaged in, but Bicker* does not seem to have been such a strong Calvinist

---

[45] H. A. E. van Gelder (1918), esp. pt 2.

either, and Blaeu* once went so far as to dedicate a book to Pope Alexander VII. Martin Coster* has been described as a 'fiery Calvinist', and he was certainly unorthodox enough to find it prudent to leave Amsterdam in 1566.[46] However, his library included not only Calvin (and not very much Calvin at that) but also works by Erasmus and Melanchthon and even the decrees of the Council of Trent. Despite the fact that he was an elder of the Calvinist church, Reynier Cant* objected to attempts to drive out the Catholics after 1578, and it was said that he died a Catholic himself.[47] Cant* also found himself called before the church authorities on account of the music and dancing at his daughter's wedding in 1584.[48]

In the controversy between Professor Arminius and Professor Gomarus over the deep points of grace and predestination which came to a head about the year 1608 it is tempting and not unreasonable to see an analogy with the Venetian crisis of 1606. In both cities the theology of grace had become entwined with a political question, whether the state was to control the church or not – or, better, whether the patricians were to control the clergy or not.

It is equally tempting, but more misleading, to take the gentle Hooft* as typical of Amsterdam patrician attitudes, in the same way that it is both tempting and misleading to take Nicolò Contarini* as typical of Venetian ones. It is true that Arminius himself had married into the patriciate – in 1590 he married Lijsbeth, daughter of Laurens Reael* (father of the more famous Admiral Dr Laurens Reael*). Other members of the elite, such as Dirck Bas* and Albert Burgh,* supported the position of the 'Remonstrants', or followers of Arminius. It is true that the Grand Pensionary of Holland, Oldenbarnevelt, supported both the Arminians and the power of the Dutch regent class; that the Prince of Orange supported the Gomarists (or 'Counter-Remonstrants') and that in 1618, when the controversy was at its height, he purged the Council of Amsterdam and other towns of supporters

[46] Evenhuis (1965–7), vol. 1, 275.
[47] Ibid., 99.
[48] Roodenburg (1990), 324.

of Arminius. It is also the case that when the Remonstrants were forced into founding a separate church, twelve members of the Amsterdam elite (not to mention their close relatives) had their children baptized there between 1633 and 1673. They included Hans Bontemantel,* whose political diary is such an important source for our knowledge of the period, Henrick Hooft* (following in the footsteps of his great-uncle, C. P. Hooft*), Nicolaes van Loon,* Willem van Loon* and Cornelis van Vlooswijk.*[49]

All this is true, but not the whole story. The Amsterdam elite no less than the Venetian contained a devout party or faction, kerkelyken (to use the contemporary term) as well as libertynen. The Prince of Orange was able to step in and purge the Town Council of Amsterdam in 1618 partly because he had allies within it. The devout faction was led by Reynier Pauw,* one of the key figures behind the convocation of the synod of Dort, where the Remonstrants were excommunicated. Unfortunately, Pauw's* papers have not survived, so that it is not possible to describe his religious attitudes in any detail.[50]

We do have some evidence from his circle, however, from Pieter Schaep* for instance. Dr Pieter Schaep* wrote a letter of advice to his son when Gerard Schaep* went up to Leiden University in 1617.[51] It is difficult to avoid the term 'puritan' when describing the cluster of attitudes expressed in this letter (some of the Dutch thought the term relevant to their society, for no less a man than Johan van Oldenbarnevelt once described the Counter-Remonstrants to the British ambassador as 'double puritans').[52] Dr Schaep* was concerned that his son should organize his studies well, that he should avoid wasting time, drunkenness and 'whoredom' and, above all, that he should 'fear God'. Quotations from Proverbs and from Ecclesiastes about the fear of the Lord echo through the letter. Gerard Schaep's* papers have also survived. The image of God which emerges from them is that of a being who intervenes constantly in daily life, a very different image from the

---

[49] Bontemantel (1897), vol. 2, lxiv.
[50] J. E. Elias (1923), 149ff; NNBW, vol. 9, cols 769–76.
[51] GA, Bicker papers, no. 717, 218–20.
[52] Carleton (1775), 100.

God of C. P. Hooft,* who liked to stress man's ignorance of the divine.[53]

Thus in Calvinist Amsterdam as in Catholic Venice there was both a devout group and an anti-clerical group within the elite. Where the fear of Spain played into the hands of the Venetian anti-clericals, in Amsterdam it played into the hands of the devout. One should perhaps interpret the stern doctrines of the synod of Dort as the expression of a mood of fear, which declined when the fear of Spain declined, in the middle of the seventeenth century. As in New England, the shift from middle-class to patrician values among the urban elite may also have contributed to the decline of Calvinism.[54] The last of the strict Calvinists in the Amsterdam regent class was probably Nicolaes Tulp,* who died in 1674 at the age of eighty-one.

One might illustrate the shift in religious attitudes in Amsterdam by contrasting two members of the Witsen family who flourished in the early and the late seventeenth century respectively. Gerrit Witsen* was a zealous Calvinist, as one might have expected from a friend of Reynier Pauw.* Nicolaes Witsen* was interested in religion but in a more ecumenical way. In Russia he went to visit patriarch Nikon and he made notes on the cult of icons, the importance of St Nicholas and other details of Orthodox worship. His sympathies extended to the 'holy Confucius', and he was also interested in shamanism.[55]

It would be unwise to take Coenraad van Beuningen* as typical of anything, but at least he illustrates another possible religious attitude of the late seventeenth century, another route away from strict Calvinism. Beuningen* opposed Catholicism, Lutheranism and Calvinism alike as the 'three unclean spirits'. His sympathies were not with churches but with sects – with the Collegianten of Rijnsburg (a circle in which Spinoza moved), the Quakers, the Behmenists (followers of Jakob Boehme) and with the followers of Labadie, another example of the 'Christians without a church' of the seventeenth century.[56]

[53] Schaep (1655).
[54] Howe (1972).
[55] Witsen (1705), 664ff; Witsen (1966–7), vol. 1, 400ff, 455ff.
[56] Roldanus (1931); Kolakowski (1965), 719–49.

8

Patronage of the Arts

The differences in the style of life, attitudes and values of the patricians of Amsterdam and Venice were reflected in their patronage of the arts.

Despite their ideal of personal frugality, Venetian patricians were believers in 'magnificence', which they defined themselves in terms of 'conspicuous consumption' (a possible if free translation of *spendere largamente*).[1] The great occasions for displaying this magnificence were 'banquets, weddings and buildings, where it is right to spend without thinking of the expense'. The point about buildings is an important one. Like clothes, they were part of the 'front' of the Venetian nobleman. The architect Vincenzo Scamozzi described the Venetian palace as an expression of 'the style of life of the nobility' (*l'uso del vivere della nobiltà*), pointing out, for example, the importance of the main entrance and the need 'to be able to give receptions for the relatives when there are weddings, and to give parties and feasts'.[2]

The dominant motive for all this magnificence was family pride, a sense of the 'honour' or 'splendour' of the 'house', its *honorevolezza, decoro, lustro, splendore*. The family palace was at the centre of the attention of patricians. They would dream for generations of enlarging it or redecorating it, buying up the neigh-

---

[1] Paruta (1579), 282; cf. Burke (1982).
[2] Scamozzi (1615), 243.

bouring houses and exhorting their descendants to carry on the good work. Thus Marin Grimani,* in his will, described the 2,844 ducats he had spent on the *soler* (upper) apartment of the palace at San Luca, built by the famous Renaissance architect Sammicheli for his father, and he instructed his heirs to have a staircase of Veronese stone made for the main entrance. The palace was more than a place to live, it was a symbol of the family. It was surely no accident that the same term, *casa*, was used of both. Hence Antonio Grimani* wrote of his palace in his will: 'I do not want it ever to be rented out; it must be inhabited by my sons and their dependants for ever.' Zuan da Lezze* gave his heirs similar instructions not to divide, sell or rent out the palace.

Some spectacular new palaces were built in seventeenth-century Venice, including Palazzo Pisani on Campo San Stefano, built when Alvise Pisani* was head of the branch, and Palazzo Pesaro on the Grand Canal, planned by Zuan Pesaro* and built for his nephew Lunardo Pesaro by Baldassare Longhena (the most famous Venetian architect of the seventeenth century). The branch had bought houses nearby in 1558, 1569 and 1628 in order to make possible a building on this scale. Similarly, Zuan da Lezze* declared in his will that he had spent over 34,000 ducats on the family palace (near the Church of the Crutched Friars) and bought the house next door with a view to future enlargements.[3]

Sumptuous monuments, built by teams of architects and sculptors, were another way of glorifying the family, or even the individual, in a way which would have been almost unimaginable in the fifteenth and sixteenth centuries. Seventeenth-century monuments quite dwarf the tombs of earlier times. The monument to Marin Grimani* at San Iseppo cost 5,865 ducats, but this was nothing compared with the monument to Silvestro Valier* at San Zanipolo, which cost 20,000. Portrait busts now in museums often derive from these tombs; the famous Vittoria bust of Nicolò da Ponte* is an example. In the later seventeenth century, in contrast to earlier Venetian practice, a patrician might decide to give his parish church a new façade and commission sculptors to turn it into an enormous family monument. Andrea Contarini, son of Carlo Contarini,* left 10,000 ducats to rebuild the façade of

San Vidal and decorate it with the busts of his parents. Vincenzo
Fini* and his brother made the façade of San Moisè into a monument to themselves at a cost of 90,000 ducats.

Even the villa in the country was turning into a palace at this
time.[4] Think, for example, of Villa Corner at Poisuolo, designed
by Scamozzi for Zuan I Corner,* of Villa Contarini at Piazzola,
enlarged by Marco Contarini,* and of the two spectacular examples from the early eighteenth century, Villa Manin at Passeriano
(for the family of Ottavio Manin*) and Villa Pisani at Strà, for the
Pisani of San Stefano, a branch of the family which contributed six
members to the elite in the period. This last villa was rebuilt on a
still grander scale in neopalladian style from 1737 onwards, and
decorated by Gianbattista Tiepolo in the 1760s with frescoes
glorifying the family. An exception to this trend was the modest
villa at Conselve near Padua built by Zuan Sagredo,* but his
meanness, as we have seen, was if not proverbial, at least anecdo-
tal. Or should one say that he kept up the ancient virtue of
frugality in an increasingly corrupt age?

The patronage of painters and writers was rather less a matter
of the honour of the house and rather more a question of personal
taste, likely to reflect a genuine interest in the arts. Marcantonio
Barbaro* not only employed Veronese to decorate his villa but
tried his hand at sculpture. Zuan Pesaro's* love of paintings even
led him to loot some on one occasion when he was in command of
Venetian forces. A visitor to the house of a Venetian patrician
would have been struck by the number of paintings, portraits most
of all. Tintoretto painted Marcantonio Barbaro,* Pasquale
Cicogna,* Polo Paruta,* Vincenzo Morosini* and other members
of the elite. Some portraits were certainly commissioned to glorify
the family. Nicolò Corner* had three portraits of his ancestress
Caterina, Queen of Cyprus, while the inventory of Francesco da
Molin's* paintings begins with six pictures of senators and generals of the da Molin family.[5]

Other portraits were there to gratify the interest in history
which, as we have seen, was a leading characteristic of the
Venetian patriciate: portraits of doges, of cardinals, the occasional

[4]   Mazzotti (1953, 1957).
[5]   Savini-Branca (1964).

pope, king or even 'the Grand Turk'. There would also be historical paintings, usually classical, like *Alexander and the Family of
Darius* or *Scipio and the Spanish Slave*, both illustrating the virtues of a conqueror: clemency and continence. These were the
private equivalents of the paintings of historical scenes in the
Doge's Palace, which were also seen as 'examples of virtue'
(*esempi virtuosi*). Giacomo Correr* had a particularly fine collection of historical paintings.

Religious paintings were also much in evidence. They consti-
tuted about a third of Ferigo Contarini's* collection (57 out of
153) as of Francesco da Molin's* (39 out of 136). St John the
Baptist, St Francis, the Magdalena and St Sebastian were among
the most popular saints, while such local favourites as St Mark,
Santa Marina and the blessed Lorenzo Giustinian (himself a
Venetian noble) also made an appearance. The rest of the collection would probably have been made up of classical mythologies,
such as paintings of Venus and Apollo, and of what contemporaries called 'moral inventions', allegorical paintings with titles like
Truth, or *Time, Prudence and Fame*. There might also be a few
landscapes in seventeenth-century Venetian collections, but they
were very much in the background of attention.

Lying on his death-bed, Zuanfrancesco Loredan is said to have
told his son, 'Among other obligations entailed on you I leave the
patronage of *virtuosi* . . . The Venetian noble has always been the
protector of literary men.'[6] Books were dedicated to members of
the elite, to a few of them (such as Nicolò Sagredo*) in particular,
and presumably the authors were rewarded. In the late seventeenth century there was a kind of unofficial poet laureate in
Venice, the priest Cristoforo Ivanovitch, who used to write regular
and (for modern tastes, at least) somewhat nauseating complimen-
tary verses on the proctors and others to celebrate their marriages
and political appointments. Thus he wrote a sonnet for the appointment of Girolamo Zustinian* when he became a proctor in
1675, with an appropriate reference to the eagle on the clan coat
of arms; a sonnet for Girolamo Grimani* when he was made
provveditore generale of Dalmatia in 1675; and many other pieces
of what Ivanovitch himself described as his 'poetic applause'.[7]

6 Lupis (1663), 41.
7 Ivanovitch (1681).

Some of the devout faction, including Agostino Barbarigo* and Zaccaria Contarini,* in the late sixteenth century wanted the theatres closed and the actors expelled from Venice. Contarini,* indeed, is said to have been carried from his sickbed to the Senate to make a speech against the actors.[8] But other patricians took a lively interest in the theatre and in music. In the later sixteenth century the amateur theatricals of the aristocratic youth groups known as the 'societies of the hose' (*compagnie delli calzi*), so called because of their colourful costumes, still existed, and Andrea Dolfin,* for instance, was a member of one of these clubs in his youth.

Marin Grimani* was an enthusiast for music, and Venice was one of the first cities in Europe to welcome the new art form of the opera. The commercial opera house (that is, one to which entry was by ticket and not by invitation) was introduced to Venice in 1637. By the late seventeenth century there were twelve opera houses in Venice, of which eight were owned by noble families, including Alvise Duodo,* who opened one at Sant' Aponal in 1651, and Marcantonio Zustinian, in whose family theatre at San Moisè Monteverdi's *Arianna* had its première in 1640.[9] Marco Contarini* had a theatre and a music-room constructed on his country estate at Piazzola on the Brenta; 120 manuscript scores now in the Marciana Library in Venice come from his famous collection, including those of 27 operas with music by Cavalli.[10] Subjects from Roman history were extremely popular, Scipio and Alexander among them. In 1595, for instance, the musical drama *The Triumph of Scipio* was played before the Doge, Marin Grimani;* in 1651 an opera called *Alexander Conqueror of Himself* was performed, in 1664, Cavalli's *Scipio Africanus*; while at the beginning of the eighteenth century Joseph Addison attended a performance of an opera about Caesar and Scipio.[11] The analogy with the paintings collected by patricians will be obvious enough.

The works of architecture and sculpture commissioned by the Amsterdam elite show, as one might have expected, less magnifi-

[8]   Cozzi (1959a); Taviani (1970), 69.
[9]   Worsthorne (1954).
[10] Wiel (1888).
[11] Addison (1705), 97ff.

cence, less display and less desire for the conspicuous glorification of the family. There were some fairly grand town houses, it is true, like the present Herengracht no. 446, the house of Andries de Graeff;* the house of Alexander Velters* on the Herengracht, valued at 40,000 florins; the Trippenhuis, a town hall in miniature; or the house Philips Vingboons built on the Singel for the Huydecoper family, which took up the space of three ordinary houses and had a magnificent garden, with fountain and statues, which gave it the appearance, from the rear, of a country house rather than a town one.[12] In general, however, the houses of the Amsterdam elite were not on the scale of the Venetian palaces, nor were they so expensive. Two houses on the Keizersgracht owned by members of the elite, Jan de Bisschop* early in the seventeenth century and Daniel Bernard* at its end, were valued at 14,000 florins each; that would be about 7,000 ducats, little enough by Venetian standards. (I omit Bernard's stabling facilities in the nearby Blomstraat, valued at another 2,500 florins.) In Amsterdam a house was simply a place for the nuclear family to live in and it does not seem to have had the symbolic importance of the Venetian palace.

Nor did the Amsterdammers spend much on family tombs. It was not that the grand tomb was unknown in the Dutch Republic: the public monuments to William the Silent and to Piet Hein are splendid instances to the contrary. All the same, the sumptuous monument was not part of the style of life of the Amsterdam elite, with occasional exceptions. The de Graeff family, predictably, had their own Chapel, the former St Cornelius chapel, in the Old Church, and Cornelis de Graeff* commissioned a tomb there with sculptures by an artist from the south, Artus Quellin.[13]

The country houses of the Amsterdam elite seem to have been modest affairs compared with those of seventeenth-century Venetians, in spite of the occasional flattering poetic reference to a 'palace'.[14] They tended to lack columns or pilasters. Most of them have disappeared, but a modest style and scale are suggested by contemporary drawings and also by the occasional valuation.

[12]   Vingboons (1688), fo. 2r.
[13]   Wagenaar (1779), 103.
[14]   Luttervelt (1943), 128.

Take Vredenhof, for example, the country house near Voors-choten which once belonged to Andries de Graeff.* In 1733 it was valued at 9,000 florins, including the gardens and other land round it. The inventory of 1733 lists the rooms. There was a 'great chamber' (*groote zaal*), but there were only eleven rooms alto-gether, including four service rooms – kitchen, cellar, servants' room and coach-house.[15]

In Amsterdam the important commissions for architects were not private but public. The great expansion of the city ensured that builders were not left unemployed. It was as burgomasters rather than as private individuals that the de Graeffs, Bickers and others handed out commissions for the South Church (1603), the West Church (1620), the Bourse and, best known of all, the new Town Hall. Like medieval Florence or medieval Venice, patronage in seventeenth-century Amsterdam was predominantly civic.

On the other hand, Amsterdam patricians seem to have equalled Venetians in their interest in collecting pictures, by the later seven-teenth century, if not before. Jan Six,* the patron of Rembrandt, is the most famous example, but there are many others. There was a similar interest in portraits in both cities. Gerard Schaep,* an enthusiast for family history, records an expense of 450 florins for having family portraits copied and framed.[16] More characteristic of Amsterdam, as of the Dutch Republic in general, was the group portrait, showing the administrators of a poor-house or hospital, or the anatomy lessons painted for physicians like Nicolaes Tulp* and Sebastiaen Egbertszoon.*[17]

More important still was another kind of group portrait, the *schutterstuk*, the painting of the civic guard in their uniforms. In the Rijksmuseum today there are ten such paintings in which the captain of the guard is one of the elite, from Jan de Bisschop* (1599) to Joan Huydecoper* (1648). These works were sometimes put on display in the *doelen* (militia headquarters), but they might hang in the captain's house. Historical paintings could also be found in the houses of patricians – Lucretia and Portia, for exam-ple, presumably as symbols of womanly virtue, and the Horatii,

15 GA, de Graeff papers, no. 608, fo. 82r.
16 GA, Bicker papers, no. 717, sect. 4, 99.
17 Heckscher (1958).

symbols of civic patriotism. Many have been lost, but the grander
collections can be reconstructed from the poems of Jan Vos, who
celebrated the deeds and possessions of the patricians in similar
style to Ivanovitch. Thanks to Vos we know that 'moral inventions' could be found in Amsterdam as well as Venice, such as the
elaborate programme executed by Nicolaes Held-Stokade for
Louys Trip,* in which Prudence, Wisdom, Fortune and Riches add
up to a pictorial panegyric to Trip's* success in business.[18]

As might have been thought, Old Testament subjects were
rather more popular in Amsterdam collections than in Venetian
ones: Abraham, for example, David, Joseph and Solomon. The
emphasis on landscape, on still life and on genre paintings was
only to be expected. It is somewhat more surprising to find the
occasional St Sebastian or St Stephen, however, or to discover that
a few burgomasters collected classical mythologies. Andries de
Graeff,* for instance, owned paintings of Ceres, Flora, Juno,
Venus and 'a naked Diana lying down'.[19] The strongly Calvinist
burgomaster Tulp* once protested against the floats of 'heathen
gods and goddesses' laid on to entertain the Prince of Orange: one
wonders what he made of his colleague's paintings.[20]

Tulp* was no enemy of the arts. He sat for at least ten portraits.
He asked the famous silversmith Janus Lutma to make a silver
goblet for him in the shape of a tulip, in allusion to his name.[21]
Rembrandt's famous *Anatomy Lesson* was painted for him, and
he was particularly fond of the work of Paul Potter, who special-
ized in painting animals in landscapes. Indeed, Tulp* invited
Potter to Amsterdam and owned most of his work.[22] This contrast
in collections between de Graeff* and Tulp* may furnish a little
support for the old argument that Calvinism indirectly encouraged
the rise of landscape painting.

Much the same small group of patricians also acted as patrons
of literature. In the early seventeenth century the 'chambers of
rhetoric', a kind of literary club, were still important in the culture
of the United Provinces. The Amsterdam chamber, De Egelantier,

[18]   Vos (1726), 380ff; cf. Worp (1879).
[19]   GA, de Graeff papers, no. 608, fos 56ff.
[20]   Fremantle (1959), 64.
[21]   Heckscher (1958), 74ff.
[22]   Houbraken (1718–21), vol. 1, 102; Cuyper (1898).

included members of such patrician families as Pauw, Reael and Schaep. The brothers de Graeff,* the Huydecopers,* father and son, and Jan Six* recur in the dedications of the works of Vondel as they do in those of Vos. Amsterdam patricians, like Venetian ones, received 'poetic applause' when they married, went on embassy or were appointed burgomasters. Poems were written about their portraits or their country houses. A vast quantity of this occasional verse was produced. For instance, at least twenty-four people celebrated in Latin verse the burgomasterships and the death of Willem Backer.*[23] As for more serious works, it is interesting to find the same mixture of biblical and classical themes in the plays written for the Amsterdam theatre as in the galleries of the Huydecopers* and the de Graeffs* – plays about David, Solomon, Medea and Claudius Civilis, the Batavian hero of resistance to Rome.

It is natural to wonder whether the patricians had any influence on the plays which were dedicated to them, and if so, what they wanted. In one case at least there is good evidence for an answer, the case of Vondel's *Palamedes*. One day in 1625, according to the church historian Geeraerd Brandt (who knew the poet personally), Vondel was talking to Albert Burgh* about Oldenbarnevelt, who had been executed six years before, and Burgh* said, 'Write about it.' Vondel answered, 'It isn't the time yet.' Burgh* replied, 'Just change the names.'[24] The result was *Palamedes*. In an age accustomed to historical parallels there was no difficulty in recognizing the 'injured innocent' Palamedes as Oldenbarnevelt, Agamemnon as Maurice, Prince of Orange, or Megeer as Reynier Pauw.* Vondel was called before the magistrates of Amsterdam to answer for his play. Some of them wanted him acquitted, while others, the devout faction, wanted him punished severely. In the end he was simply fined.

This was not the only occasion that Vondel ran into trouble for his plays. In 1638 the church council (*kerkeraad*) complained that his play *Gysbrecht van Amstel* was 'superstitious'. Set in the Middle Ages, it contained references to Catholic beliefs. Despite the complaint, burgomaster Jacob de Graeff* declared that there

---

[23] GA, Backer papers, no. 70.
[24] Brandt (1682), 14.

was nothing offensive in it and the performance went ahead. Again, in 1654, the church council complained about Vondel's *Lucifer*. This time the burgomasters (one of whom was Tulp*) banned the play. The divergences between the de Graeff family and Tulp* extended to their attitudes to the drama.

The Town Council was divided not only about Vondel, it was divided on the question of whether to have a theatre at all. The devout faction (like the English puritans in this respect too) wanted the theatre closed and the building turned into a school. The burgomasters tended to take a moderate line, supporting the existence of the theatre but warning the players against causing scandal. This moderation seems to have been the resultant of opposing forces. For example, in 1666, a year when the burgomasters allowed the theatre to reopen but gave the actors a stern warning, the burgomasters included Tulp* but also Vondel's patrons Cornelis van Vlooswijk* and Andries de Graeff.*[25]

Much has been written about the possible relationship between the Counter-Reformation and the baroque style, and something about Calvinism and classicism. A comparative study of the taste of two seventeenth-century patriciates, one Catholic and one predominantly Calvinist, seems an obvious way of attacking the problem.

In Venice there were influential patricians of sober tastes in the late sixteenth century, Ferigo Contarini* and Lunardo Donà for example.[26] However, the taste for the ornate soon became dominant. Tintoretto had been a controversial painter, but in the next generation his follower Sante Peranda became quite fashionable for religious paintings. Peranda's style was admired at the time for its grace and elegance, his *maniera cosi graziosa, gentile e leggiadra*, and his patrons included such prominent members of the devout faction as Marin Grimani,* who took him to Rome in 1592, and Renier Zen,* who owned an *Agony in the Garden* and a *Scourging at the Pillar*.[27] For portraits, the man was Tiberio Tinelli, a painter much influenced by Van Dyck. Antonio Nani* and Antonio Priuli* owned works by Tinelli. Another fashionable

---

[25]   Kalff (1895); Worp (1904–8), vol. 2, 99ff.
[26]   O. Logan (1972), 192; Tafuri (1985), ch. 1.
[27]   Quotation from Boschini (1664), Introduction.

painter of the time was Pietro Liberi, a pupil of Padovanino. Francesco da Molin* admired Liberi's work and had the painter knighted in 1652, while the Fini* family commissioned him to decorate their palace and Alvise Pisani* and Giacomo Correr* each owned a painting by him.[28] Correr* also owned a work by the 'capricious' Joseph Heinz and a 'strangely beautiful painting' (*pittura pelegrina*) by Luca Ferrari.[29]

Turning to sculpture, we find that the most famous of baroque statues, Bernini's St Teresa, was commissioned by a Venetian patrician, Cardinal Ferigo Corner, son of Doge Zuan I Corner.* Tirali's monument to Silvestro Valier* (1705–8) includes the whole baroque apparatus of draperies, swags and coloured marble. It was Vincenzo Fini* who commissioned the façade of San Moisè from the architect Tremignon and the sculptor Meyring, a Flemish follower of Bernini. Richness of decoration could hardly go further. The columns on the façade of San Moisè are not only fluted, they have ornamental bands across them, and these bands are themselves ornamented with rosettes. It may be significant that new nobles were responsible for this spectacular lapse from the Venetian tradition of sobriety.

More eclectic in his tastes was Doge Nicolò Sagredo.* His will refers to some of his paintings, including two 'in the room in which I sleep', a Pietro di Cortona and a Poussin. The taste for Poussin seems an unusual one in a Venetian patrician of the period; perhaps it resulted from Sagredo's* residence in Rome as ambassador in the 1650s. It was in Rome that he came to appreciate the work of the baroque painter Carlo Maratta, from whom he commissioned an *Adoration of the Magi*.[30]

From about 1640 onwards the rising taste for the exuberant can be illustrated by opera, which in this period was spectacle, drama and music – in that order. In literature the Venetian elite were split between the taste for the ornate and difficult and the taste for the plain and simple. Pietro Basadonna* was said to be 'a lover of conceits and of pungent witticisms' (*amico delle arguzie e de'concettini frizzanti*).[31] Zuanfrancesco Loredan was a great ad-

[28] Savini-Branca (1964).
[29] Boschini (1660), 553.
[30] Bellori (1672), 586–7.
[31] RA, 384.

mirer of the baroque poet Marino, whose biography he wrote, and
he cultivated what contemporaries would have called a 'conceited'
style himself. A taste for the exotic is to be found both in the
subjects for operas and romances and in their treatment. An inflation (not to say debasement) of language was taking place; the
word 'heroic' is an obvious example of this process, especially
when it rolls off the pen of Cristoforo Ivanovitch, describing (for
instance) the erection of a theatre at Piazzola as the result of the
'heroic genius'and the 'heroic generosity' of Marco Contarini.*
Playing on words was popular, as it was elsewhere in baroque
Europe, and word-play turns up in the most serious contexts.
When Domenico Contarini* refers in his will to his brother's
'angelic virtues', it may come as a surprise to the modern reader to
discover that his brother's name was Angelo.

Other Venetians, like Paolo Sarpi and his circle, including
Nicolò Contarini* and Lunardo Donà,* wrote in a simple style.
They were not alone in their tastes. The Senate did not care for
Basadonna's* speeches because it preferred a 'solid and vigorous
style' (le sode e vigorose sentenze) to a sharp and conceited one.[32]
It was also the Senate which voted for Longhena's plan for the
Church of the Salute, a plan described to them by the building
committee not in terms of mass or ornament but in terms of
spaciousness and light.[33] It is tempting to see the taste for the
simple as corresponding to the traditional Venetian style of frugality and the taste for the ornate as associated with the new style of
more conspicuous consumption. In the seventeenth century the
ornate style was winning.

In Amsterdam the plain style seems to have been dominant
throughout the period, in the architecture of Vingboons and Van
Campen, the landscapes of Potter, the flower pieces of Van
Huysum or the portraits of Van de Helst. Van de Helst seems to
have been the most fashionable portrait painter for the Amsterdam elite between the 1640s and the 1660s; his sitters included
Daniel Bernard,* Frans Banningh Cocq* (who is best known for
his appearance in Rembrandt's more flamboyant Night Watch),
Joan Huydecoper,* Albert Pater,* Cornelis de Vlooswijk* and

[32] RA, 386.
[33] Moschini (1842), 7ff.

Cornelis Witsen.* His works are perceptive but they do not seem to idealize their subjects. In this sense we may agree with Jan Romein's application of the Marxian category of 'bourgeois realism' to the paintings commissioned by the regent class.[34] The artist and writer Houbraken specifically mentions the lack of ornament on the houses designed by Philips Vingboons, for example the house he built at Pijnenburgh near Utrecht for the widow of Jacob Hinlopen.*[35]

A small group of patricians seems to have been attracted by a grander style. Rembrandt worked for a number of them, especially the Arminians.[36] The brothers Trip, Louys* and Nicolaes,* had their aged parents Jacob and Margareta painted by Rembrandt. The old-fashioned clothes of the couple, especially Margareta's ruff, have often been noted. Was this an indicator of her old-fashioned tastes, or a way of lending the family an air of antiquity? In any case, Jacob, with his air of an Old Testament patriarch, makes a splendid ancestor. Andries de Graeff* – besides sitting to Rembrandt and quarrelling over the price – employed the painter Jacob Jordaens and the sculptor Artus Quellin, both baroque in style and, significantly, from Antwerp. He was also on friendly terms with the painter Govert Flinck, who borrowed elegant poses from Van Dyck to make his sitters look more aristocratic. Flinck painted a portrait of an unidentified member of the Munter family (which contributed four members to the elite), in which the sitter has one hand to his breast and the other elegantly drooping.[37]

Coenraed van Beuningen,* eccentric as usual, fits neither category; his tastes in painting were for Dürer and for the Flemish landscape painter Herri met de Bles.[38] But the general impression left by Amsterdam patrician taste is predominantly sober with a dash of something grander, an impression summed up by the Town Hall, a plain building whose simple lines do not harmonize with the enormous pediments full of allegorical sculpture, again the work of Artus Quellin.

[34] Romein (1934), 419.
[35] Houbraken (1718-21), vol. 3, 402.
[36] Dudok van Heel (1969), 149ff; Schwartz (1985).
[37] Moltke (1965), nos 201, 205, 206, 424, 476, 477.
[38] Roldanus (1931), 57n.

The taste for the difficult in literature seems to have been more widespread than the taste for the ornate in painting. Puns, anagrams and acrostics were all popular in the literature addressed to the elite. For Pieter Schaep* (Petrus Schaepius) someone composed the anagram *tu spe hic superas*.[39] When Vos wrote an epitaph on Abraham Boom,* he could not resist the obvious reference to a tree (*boom*), and his epitaph on Albert Burgh* calls him the 'people's stronghold' (*Burgerburg*). Nor could he describe Marsseveen, the villa of his chief patron, Joan Huydecoper,* without a flattering pun on 'Mars and Venus'.[40] This show of learning and ingenuity suggests a conscious attempt on the part of the patriciates of Venice, Amsterdam and elsewhere (Barcelona, for example) to distance themselves from ordinary people and so affirm their aristocratic status.[41]

---

[39]   GA, Bicker papers, no. 717, sect. 4, 222.
[40]   Vos (1726), 399.
[41]   Cf. Amelang (1986), ch. 8.

9

From Entrepreneurs to Rentiers

In every chapter so far there have been references to changes over time. These changes deserve a chapter to themselves, describing the differences between the patricians of Amsterdam and Venice in 1580 and the patricians of those two cities in 1720. The obvious question to ask, one which has been asked ever since the seventeenth century itself, is whether Venice and Amsterdam 'declined'. 'Decline' is a concept which historians would find it difficult to do without, but it is, none the less, a rather vague term. It is necessary to make all sorts of distinctions before one can use it with confidence. Did the cities of Venice and Amsterdam decline or did their elites decline? Was the decline a fall in numbers, a fall in wealth or a fall in power? Was the decline absolute or relative?

Let us look at numbers first. In Venice, where the elite was the upper part of a formally defined nobility, demographic decline was visible enough. The Venetian noblemen over twenty-five (that is, of an age to join the Greater Council) numbered 1,967 in 1594, but their numbers had diminished to 1,703 by the year 1719. A hundred new families had joined the nobility in the meantime, adding 316 individuals over twenty-five in 1719, so the decline in the older families was a steep one, from 1,967 to 1,387. It should be added that the new families lacked the clan organization of the old ones; the new families in 1719 averaged three adult males per surname, the old families averaged twelve.[1]

---

[1] For 1594, BCV, MS Donà 225; for 1719, BCV, MS Cicogna 913.

One reason for this decline in numbers was plague, in particular the plague of 1630–1 (since the choice of 1580 as a base-line means that the effects of the other great plague, that of 1575–7, have already been taken into account). Venice as a whole recovered from the plague in the sense that its population went up again to its former level, about 140,000. The nobility, on the other hand, did not. It may be that Venice recovered its former size only as a result of immigration, and that families of native-born Venetians were generally reduced in numbers; there has been no study of this problem. In the case of the nobility, however, historians have been attracted by one explanation given at the time, that the numbers of nobles were falling because fewer of them were marrying. A case-study of twenty-one Venetian noble families has shown that in the sixteenth century 51 per cent of noblemen reaching marriageable age did not marry; in the seventeenth century the proportion rose to 60 per cent, and in the eighteenth century it would rise to 66 per cent. The same study also remarks on the fact that 40 per cent of marriages produced only one child or no child at all, and explained this by the prevalence of gonorrhoea among the patriciate – but as a critic has pointed out, children who died in infancy were not always recorded in the sources.[2]

Another change in the structure of the Venetian nobility was the local equivalent to the 'inflation of honours' well known for seventeenth-century England. During the wars with the Ottoman Empire over Crete, in the middle of the century, and over the Morea, towards its end, the government was in great need of money. It therefore decided to allow new families to join the nobility at the price of 100,000 ducats.[3] Even a family who sold sausages and came from Bergamo (the Minelli) was acceptable to the government at that price, a fact which caused great bitterness among the nobles of old stock. It also became easier to buy proctorships, for 20,000 or 25,000 ducats. There were about twice as many proctors in 1719 as there had been in 1578, and some of them had held no other important offices. What is especially striking, in a gerontocracy like Venice, is the selling of five

[2] Rodenwalt (1957); Davis (1962), 62.
[3] Cowan (1985, 1986).

proctorships to teenagers, one in 1649 to the Doge's son, Silvestro Valier,* and the other four in the 1690s, when lack of men to fill offices as well as lack of money was becoming an acute problem for the Venetian government. However, the old noble families virtually monopolized these honours. Only five members of new families became proctors in the period.

In the Dutch Republic the patriciates of some towns, Zierikzee for example, faced problems of declining numbers not unlike that of Venice, but Amsterdam was not one of them.[4] The city continued to grow until about 1680, and the number of offices to be filled was small compared with Venice. In fact the tendency in Amsterdam in the late seventeenth century was for the elite to close up. Of forty new burgomasters chosen between 1696 and 1748, only three were not related to previous burgomasters. There was no decline in power for families like the Corvers.

The patricians of Venice and Amsterdam do not seem to have declined in wealth during the period. In Venice in 1581 the eighteen members of the elite who filled in returns of their income averaged 1,300 ducats a year, and in 1711 the thirty-eight who filled in returns averaged 7,500 ducats a year. It is difficult to know quite what to make of these figures. It is unlikely that they represent a simple increase of nearly six-fold in the wealth of the Venetian upper nobility. One has to allow something for the fall in the value of money, at least from 1581 to about 1620; and something for the fact that the increasing sale of proctorships drew rich men into the elite. One may also suspect, without being able to verify the hypothesis, that the difference in incomes declared in 1581 and 1711 is very largely the difference between a group which has a good deal of capital invested in trade (capital which does not appear in the returns) and a group which derives the bulk of its income from the ownership of land and houses. Even so the elite does not seem to be in economic decline; it was not the elite but the lower nobility which became poorer.[5] It was the city which declined, from a port of European importance to a port of regional importance. And even then, it was not so much that Venice changed as that Venice stayed the same while the world around it

---

[4] Dijk and Roorda (1971).
[5] Davis (1962), ch. 2.

changed. The Dutch and English began to compete with Venice in the Mediterranean, and the Mediterranean declined because of the new importance of the Atlantic.

In Amsterdam the spectacular increase in the wealth of the richest citizens (including the elite) was real as well as apparent. Amsterdam was not a rich or populous city in 1585, when the population was around 30,000 and only 65 households had their property assessed at 10,000 florins or more. It had become both populous and rich by 1674, when the total number of inhabitants was nearing 200,000 and 259 households were assessed at 100,000 florins or more. The wealth of the city continued to increase beyond the limits of our period (to about the year 1730), and the elite continued to have a good share in that wealth.

Where, then, is the decline? Was there one? What most impressed contemporaries was a change in the style of life of the two elites. They often interpreted this change as a moral decline, though for us it is more useful to view it as a change – to revert to the language of Pareto – from a group of entrepreneurs to a group of rentiers.[6] Did this change really take place? If so, when did it happen, and why? It is convenient to begin with the seventeenth-century answers to these questions. About 1612 the British ambassador Dudley Carleton described the Venetian nobility as follows:

> They here change their manners . . . Their former course of life was merchandising; which is now quite left and they look to landward buying house and lands, furnishing themselves with coach and horses, and giving themselves the good time with more show and gallantry than was wont . . . their wont was to send their sons upon galleys into the Levant to accustom them to navigation and to trade. They now send them to travel and to learn more of the gentleman than the merchant.[7]

In 1620 an anonymous contemporary, writing in Italian, suggested that the Venetian nobles now stayed at home idly instead of travelling to the Levant and that they had turned to the exploita-

[6]   Stella (1956); Cozzi (1958), ch. 1; G. W. Kernkamp (1897), vol. 1, 107ff; Ravesteyn (1906), 186.
[7]   Carleton (1992), 27 (spelling modernized).

tion of the lands of the mainland, at the expense of their subjects there.[8]

As for the Netherlands, the Dutch historian Lieuwe van Aitzema records the complaint, made at Amsterdam in 1652, 'that the regents were not merchants, that they did not take risks on the seas but derived their income from houses, lands and securities [*renten*], and so allowed the sea to be lost'. The passage has been quoted many times in discussions of Dutch social history in the last hundred years.[9] In other words, contemporaries remarked a very important shift in the style of life of the two elites in the course of the seventeenth century. The shift was from sea to land, from work to play, from thrift to conspicuous consumption, from entrepreneur to rentier, from bourgeois to aristocrat.

Before going on to discuss explanations for this shift, we had better take the excellent advice of the seventeenth-century scholar John Selden. 'The reason of a thing is not to be enquired after, till you are sure the thing itself is so. We commonly are at what's the reason of it? before we are sure of the thing.'[10] Did a shift from trade to land really take place? Contemporaries are not always right about social processes in the countries they visit or even in the countries in which they live. In the early sixteenth century a diarist from the Venetian noble clan of the Priuli had already complained in much the same terms as Carleton that the Venetian nobility was deserting the sea for the land and preferring pleasure to work. About 1600 the Venetian *capitano* of Padua declared that a third of the land in the Padovano was owned by Venetians – but the same statement had been made before, in 1446.[11] Indeed, Venetians had already bought considerable amounts of land near Padua by the end of the thirteenth century.[12] Come to that, Venetian nobles owned land on the north Italian mainland in the ninth century.[13] Thus the shift from entrepreneur to rentier begins to sound something like the rise of the middle class; it is described

[8] Relatione 2, fo. 144.
[9] Aitzema (1657–68), vol. 3, 762; cf. Brugmans (1897–1905), 158, and Renier (1944), 105.
[10] Selden (1892), 161.
[11] Beltrami (1961), 52.
[12] Cracco (1967), 82.
[13] Luzzatto (1958), 35.

as happening in so many periods that one begins to wonder whether it ever happened at all.

As for Amsterdam, the historians who have quoted the famous passage from Aitzema have not always remembered that it does not represent the considered verdict of this sober-minded and meticulous chronicler. He records it as a complaint made by some Amsterdam merchants in the first year of the first Anglo-Dutch war to the effect that the war was not being prosecuted firmly enough and that their interests were being neglected. They were making a political case, not trying to describe social change. In fact, if one looks at the occupations of the members of the Town Council in 1652, it is to find that eighteen out of the thirty-seven were merchants or manufacturers, and another eight were directors of the VOC or the WIC, leaving only eleven men who were neither, of whom the best known was burgomaster Cornelis de Graeff.* They can hardly be said to have deserted trade or to have given up taking risks.

Another approach to the problem of whether the shift from entrepreneur to rentier really occurred is to look at specific families. This is not easy to do for Venice, where information about the trading activities of nobles is so scrappy, though one might contrast Zuanbattista Donà, merchant to the Levant, with his son Lunardo Donà,* whose wealth was derived in the main from lands in the neighbourhood of Verona.[14]

The study of changes within individual families has been taken much further in the case of Amsterdam. For example, historians like to point to three generations of the de Graeff family. Dirck Graeff* was an iron-merchant, who became a burgomaster in 1578. His son Jacob was also a merchant, but he bought the manor of Zuidpolsbroek and styled himself Jacob de Graeff,* Vrijheer van Zuidpolsbroek. He was burgomaster from 1613 onwards. Two of Jacob's sons were the famous brothers Andries and Cornelis de Graeff.* They were not merchants at all but rentiers and politicians. Nicolaes Elias Pickenoy's famous portrait of Cornelis de Graeff* shows him dressed as a gentleman in a brocade doublet with lace collar and cuffs, not in a merchant's gown.

[14]   Seneca (1959), 7.

Again, one can look at three generations of the celebrated Bicker family. Gerrit Bicker,* who became burgomaster in 1603, was a brewer. His son, Andries Bicker,* who became burgomaster in 1627, was a merchant in the Russia trade. He had an estate and used the title Heer van Engelenberg, but his portrait, by Van de Helst, shows him plainly dressed and severe in expression. Dutch historians like to contrast this portrait with one of Andries Bicker's son Gerard, who looks fat and dissolute and in fact came to nothing. Another well-known contrast in lives and portraits is that between C. P. Hooft,* merchant and burgomaster, in his long sober gown, and his son P. C. Hooft, historian and poet, who did not follow his father into trade or city politics but lived like a gentleman in the castle of Muiden.

All these changes in life-style over two or three generations are clear enough, and more examples could be given, but it is important not to confuse what is happening to a family with what is happening to a social group. The Graafland family, for instance, showed the same pattern of social mobility and changing style of life as the de Graeffs, but a full century later. Cornelis Graafland,* the first of his family to enter the Town Council, was an iron-merchant, just like Dirck Graeff.* He was the son of an immigrant to Amsterdam, a chest-maker who came from Rotterdam. Cornelis Graafland entered the Council in 1667. His son Joan Graafland,* born in 1652, went to university, married into the Valckenier family, one of the most famous in the patriciate of Amsterdam, and became a burgomaster in 1703. His son Gillis Graafland* became Heer van Mijnden, where he owned a country house.

The moral is that it is not enough to take individual examples; to study the problem of 'aristocratization', or the shift from entrepreneur to rentier, it is necessary to adopt a more quantitative approach. Two facts about the elite which lend themselves to measurement are whether or not they have an occupation and whether or not they have a country house. The entrepreneur is more likely to have an occupation but no country house; the rentier to have a country house but no occupation. The rule is not infallible; if the differences between the two groups are defined in terms of attitude, it is perfectly possible to find an entrepreneur landowner (such as Jacob Poppen*), as well as rentier without a place in the country. All the same, the chances are that an increase in the ownership of country houses and a decrease in recorded occupations between them indicate a shift from entrepreneur to rentier. The trend is as follows:[15]

Period	Without occupation (%)	With country house (%)
1618–50	33	10
1650–72	66	41
1672–1702	55	30
1702–48	73	81

These figures suggest that a shift did take place but also that it was gradual, not sudden, and that the rentier became predominant around 1700 rather than around 1650 (as the Aitzema quotation suggests). The shift seems to have been associated with the increasing interest in the arts described in the previous chapter.

It is unfortunate that a similar quantitative approach cannot be attempted in the case of Venice, but all the patricians owned land at the beginning of the period as well as at its end. Since they were all noble, they did not describe their employment. Although some of them engaged in trade, directly or indirectly, the tax returns offer no information about it. All the same, there is some evidence for a shift out of trade into land in this period.[16]

There were forces pushing the Venetian elite out of trade as well as forces pulling them into land. The loss of Cyprus in 1570 was a blow to trade. Something of its impact on the elite can be gauged from the case of Francesco Corner,* who owned sugar plantations on the island. He was making his will when news of the loss reached him and he had to change some of his dispositions. Another problem for Venetian merchants was the arrival of English and Dutch ships, combining trade and piracy, in the Mediterranean and the Adriatic from about 1580 onwards. So was the arrival of the Barbary pirates and of the Uskoks, who operated

---

[15] Dijk and Roorda (1971).
[16] Woolf (1962); Davis (1975), 35ff.

from bases on the Dalmatian coast. Yet another blow to trade was the failure of the last private bank, owned by members of the Pisani and Tiepolo clans, in 1584.[17]

As for the pull towards land, there is the fact that wheat prices trebled in Venice between 1550 and 1590. Ordinary Venetians did eat wheat; the people protested against millet loaves in 1570. The growing power of the Ottoman Empire endangered corn imports from Eastern Europe, and so made it increasingly good business to grow corn on the mainland.[18]

For these reasons it is likely that Venetian nobles, including members of the elite, moved their investments into land in the late sixteenth and early seventeenth centuries, while retaining the active attitudes of entrepreneurs. There was a burst of land reclamation on the Venetian mainland in this period, in which noble consortia were predominant, consortia which included such members of the elite as Ferigo Contarini* and Luca Michiel.* By 1636 Venetians owned 38 per cent of the Padovano, compared with 33 per cent in 1600.[19] However, the land boom did not last. The economic depression of the seventeenth century, which affected most of Europe, was already noticeable in the Veneto in the 1610s, and in 1630–1 it was reinforced by plague, which quickly reduced the population under Venetian rule from about 1.7 million to about 1 million. The rural population had recovered by 1690 or thereabouts, but it is difficult to resist the impression that by that time the great Venetian landowners were taking less interest in their estates as enterprises than before.

That they had developed rentier attitudes is suggested by other kinds of evidence. It was in the late 1620s that Renier Zen* delivered a famous speech against trade in the Greater Council.[20] Antonino Colluraffi's early-seventeenth-century treatise on the education of a Venetian nobleman warned his readers against trade as a distraction from the more important business of politics.[21] An anonymous treatise of the same period sometimes attributed to Fra Paolo Sarpi also recommends nobles to keep out of

---

[17]   Tenenti (1961); Cipolla (1975).
[18]   Aymard (1966), ch. 1.
[19]   Beltrami (1961), 61.
[20]   Cozzi (1958), 229ff.
[21]   Colluraffi (1623–33), vol. 1, 179.

trade.[22] In the late seventeenth century a treatise by the Cretan nobleman Zuanantonio Muazzo comments on the shift from trade to land and explains it by a desire for more secure, if smaller incomes.[23]

The evidence from the design of villas points in the same direction. The architect Vincenzo Scamozzi distinguished between two kinds of villa: the smaller villa, where the farm is close to the owner's living quarters so that he can easily see what is going on, and the larger villa, where the living quarters are quite isolated from the rest.[24] From Villa Maser, which belonged to Marcantonio Barbaro* (died 1595) and in which the stables and the rooms for wine-making are part of the central ensemble, to Villa Manin or Villa Pisani at Strà, where there are no farm-buildings near the living quarters, the trend is clear enough. The villa-farm was replaced by the villa-palace. The rise in importance of the steward or manager, already discussed (p. 60 above), is part of the same shift.

In short, it seems as though the change from entrepreneur attitudes to rentier attitudes was a general one in both elites. In Venice it took place about 1630, and in Amsterdam towards 1700 – in each case the shift should be dated later than has usually been customary.

But why did this shift take place at all? There are two obvious possibilities which need to be discussed: explanations in terms of external and internal factors. In each case the explanation will offer an example of what Fernand Braudel called 'unconscious history', in the sense that the two elites never intended to change their attitudes or their style of life.[25] An occasional seventeenth-century Venetian, like Michele Foscarini or Zuanantonio Muazzo, might notice the decline of noble marriages and even relate this to the decline of trade, but it is unlikely that this entered into the calculations of the individuals and families concerned. There are not many societies where men as they act can see themselves as forming part of a general social trend. At the same time, it should

22   Sarpi (1788), 27.
23   Davis (1962), 43n.
24   Scamozzi (1615), 285ff; cf. Barbieri (1969).
25   Braudel (1958).

be stressed that the changes we are discussing were not imposed on the two groups by necessity; there were other possible reactions or possible strategies for them. A given patrician did not have to buy land or invest in the public debt; he did this because it seemed the wisest course at the time. He knew why he was taking this decision, but he was not aware of all its consequences, for his own family and the families of his contemporaries who were making similar decisions at the same time.

One possible explanation of the shift from entrepreneur to rentier is one in terms of internal factors. The essence of the process was summed up by Adam Smith when he wrote that 'merchants are commonly ambitious of becoming country gentlemen'.[26] Merchants were entrepreneurs, in other words they were a group oriented towards achievement. However, they were not the group with the highest status in society and they often took the highest group, the nobility, as a 'reference group' or cultural model. The nobility, on the other hand, were rentiers. So, in preindustrial Europe a successful bourgeois would tend to turn into a nobleman, or his son or grandson would do so. It is not difficult to illustrate this process from the history of England, France or Spain in the sixteenth and seventeenth centuries. Merchants would buy land, acquire titles and then leave trade. From this point of view, what is surprising is not the shift but the fact that it was delayed so long in both Venice and Amsterdam. To explain this delay one might note that both cities were located in republics, where there were no kings with court nobilities to imitate, and also that both cities were far away from good land, so that the two elites were almost forced into more productive investments. These obstacles could only delay the shift. They could not prevent it altogether.

This explanation seems to work quite well for Amsterdam. In the Dutch Republic the Amsterdam elite was not the group of highest status. Although there was no king, there was a nobility surrounding the stadholder at his court at The Hague, which could act as a reference group for the Amsterdam merchants.[27] The merchant might change his own style of life. A mission abroad might lead to his being knighted by a foreign monarch. The

[26] Smith (1776), bk 3, ch. 4.
[27] Cf. Nierop (1984).

temptation to live in a style appropriate to his knighthood was a considerable one. If he did not change his own life-style, as (for example) Sir Reynier Pauw* apparently did not, he might still want his children to do better than himself socially and bring them up to do so, sending them to the Athenaeum or to university. At least three of the elite took their doctorates and then went into trade: Dr Cornelis van Dronckelaer,* Dr Jan ten Grootenhuys* and Dr Gerard van Hellemont.* These men were *mercatores sapientes* indeed, in the style recommended by Barlaeus, but they were exceptional. In general, higher education unfitted men to follow their fathers into the family business.

The social mechanism is a well-known one. The Medici are a famous example, and it is fascinating to find the poet P. C. Hooft, son of a merchant-burgomaster, writing a book on the rise and the disasters of the Medici in which he contrasted Cosimo, who was rich and intelligent but not well educated in a formal sense, with his grandson Lorenzo 'the Magnificent', a patron of literature and a poet who was not interested in business. It is difficult to resist the impression that Hooft was thinking of his father and himself.[28] The process could not be summed up more elegantly and more brutally than in an eighteenth-century Japanese *haiku*:

> House for sale
> He writes in fine Chinese style
> The third generation.[29]

In the case of Venice, however, this kind of explanation does not work so well. The Venetian elite were part of a formally defined nobility. They had no reference group outside themselves, at least in the Middle Ages. Then, in the fifteenth century, they acquired a land empire, in northern Italy. Gradually the Venetian nobles came to buy more and more land and they also came to resemble the nobles of the mainland in their style of life and in their values. As China assimilated the invading Mongols and

[28] P. C. Hooft (1649), 5ff, 22.
[29] Dore (1965), 218.

Manchus, so the mainland of north Italy assimilated the invading Venetians. Land began as a servant but it ended as a master.

This argument about the economic consequences of a change in attitudes or mentalities has been criticized in an interesting article by an American economic historian, Richard Rapp. Rapp argues that if the profits of trade fall below the return from land, 'we do not need a change in mentality to explain the shift in investment priorities'. However, he admits that in this period `returns to commerce remained somewhat higher than for agriculture'. The reason the Venetians turned to land was to take fewer risks. This is just my point. The shift from a greater to a lesser propensity to take risks in the search for profit is precisely a shift from an entrepreneurial mentality to that of a rentier.[30]

In Amsterdam internal factors seem to explain the curve of development within individual families such as the de Graeffs or the Bickers or the Hoofts, but they do not explain changes in the group as a whole. In Venice we have already been driven to offer some kind of external explanation. The most obvious explanation of social change in terms of external factors involves looking more closely at the economy. As Pareto put it, periods of economic growth are favourable to entrepreneur elites, while periods of economic stagnation or depression are favourable to rentiers. If a period of growth is followed by a period of depression, there are two possibilities: either the ruling group will modify its attitudes and behaviour or it will be replaced by another group.

A classic formulation of the dilemma comes in a famous novel about nineteenth-century Sicily, *The Leopard*, in which a younger-generation aristocrat, Tancredi, tells an older-generation aristocrat, Fabrizio, 'If we want to keep everything as it is, it will be necessary to change everything' (*se vogliamo che tutto rimanga come è, bisogna che tutto cambi*).[31] Adaptation to a changing situation is not always as conscious as in this imaginary instance, but it might be argued that in economic hard times a natural reaction is one of contempt for trade. In other words not only a shift in investments but a change in social attitudes as well. Throughout Europe, with the exception of the Duch Republic, the

---

[30]   Rapp (1979).
[31]   Tomasi (1958), 24.

seventeenth century was an age of economic depression or crisis, so it is not surprising to find the shift from entrepreneur to rentier taking place.[32] In Venice, described by one historian as having passed through a long commercial crisis between 1602 and 1669, this explanation does seem rather plausible.[33] In fact a vicious circle was in operation. Since trade was declining, the nobles moved out of it, and since the nobles were moving out of it, trade declined. When Addison visited Venice at the beginning of the eighteenth century, he suggested that Venetian trade was falling off because on the one hand 'their nobles think it below their quality to engage in traffic', while on the other 'the merchants that are grown rich buy their nobility and generally give over trade'.[34]

In Amsterdam it is necessary to be rather more cautious. The Dutch economy in general did quite well until about 1730, when the Dutch finally lost their famous intermediary position on which their prosperity had rested. What did decline in Amsterdam was the Baltic grain trade. In the late sixteenth and early seventeenth centuries Amsterdammers played an important entrepreneurial role in importing grain from Poland and elsewhere in Eastern Europe and selling it in the Netherlands or re-exporting it to Italy, Spain and elsewhere. C. P. Hooft,* for example, had been involved in this trade. In 1631 the price of Prussian rye in Amsterdam reached its peak: 263 florins per last. Thereafter it sank, and wheat prices followed suit. This decline was counteracted by the rise of the East Indies trade, but the period 1650–70 was still (to judge from the decline in income from the 'convoys and licences') a period of decline in Amsterdam trade as a whole. At this point Jan de Witt was making investment in the public debt an attractive proposition. So where the Venetian elite moved from trade into land, the Amsterdammers began to move from trade into bonds.[35]

These explanations are far from complete. In Amsterdam it is also necessary to take into account the rise in the amount of business transacted in the Town Council; to be a regent was becoming more of a full-time job, incompatible with an active

[32] Hobsbawm (1954); Parker and Smith (1978).
[33] Sella (1961).
[34] Addison (1705), 83ff; cf. Molmenti (1919), 313.
[35] Brugmans (1897–1905); Schöffer (1964); Faber (1966); Dillen (1970).

interest in trade. If rulers need to have charisma, then one might say that the use of titles by the Amsterdam elite and their more gentlemanly style of life had a political function; the 'unheroic bourgeois', as Joseph Schumpeter called him, had to turn gentleman to be obeyed.[36] There remains the problem of relating changes of attitude within families to changes within groups. This problem is not too serious in Venice, where the proctors of 1720 were drawn from more or less the same clans as the proctors of 1580. It is much greater in Amsterdam, where new families entered the city and the elite in the course of the seventeenth century.

The problem has a solution, however. The link between changes in the attitudes of specific families and in the elite as a whole is a demographic one. In seventeenth-century Europe there was not only economic stagnation but a halt in the growth of population. There was in fact another vicious circle in operation, since hard times led to increased celibacy and later marriage (couples could not afford to marry), but these reinforced population decline which in turn made times harder (because demand for products then decreased). This demographic decline hit Amsterdam late because immigration as well as natural increase had been pushing up her population. From 1580 to 1680 there was continuous immigration into Amsterdam, including men with capital, skills and ambition. A number of these immigrants, as we have seen, entered the elite, and in other cases their sons did so.

This continued immigration was, I should like to suggest, the main reason for the survival of entrepreneur attitudes in Amsterdam. When the process of 'aristocratization' pushed the de Graeffs out of trade, other families, like the Graaflands, came to take their place. About 1680, however, Amsterdam stopped growing. The open frontier of opportunity closed at last. After 1672 (when two were inserted by the Prince of Orange), only one first-generation immigrant entered the Amsterdam elite, which naturally became predominantly rentier in composition.

The republics of Venice and the United Provinces continued to exist until the end of the eighteenth century, but from the point of view of the social historian, a cycle of important changes had been completed by about the year 1720.

[36] Schumpeter (1943), 137.

Appendix

The Investments of the Amsterdam Elite

IN THE EARLY SEVENTEENTH CENTURY

The property of J. P. Reael,* who died in 1621, was broken down as follows: 46% cash; 28% in houses; 12% in stock or voyages; 8% in bonds (including a private loan); and 6% in land (GA, Weeskamer, Div. Mem. vol. 3, fo. 110).

Jacob Poppen,* who died in 1624, had about 55% of his wealth invested in land, 33% in bonds and 11% in houses (Ravesteyn, 1906, 331ff).

Barthold Cromhout* died in 1624, leaving just over 50% of his wealth invested in land (Ravesteyn, 1906, 276ff).

Jan Bal* (alias Huydecoper) died in 1624, leaving 66% of his wealth invested in houses, 24% in land and 10% in bonds (GA, Weeskamer, Div. Mem. vol. 3, fo. 212).

Simon de Rijck* died in 1652, leaving over 70% of his wealth invested in houses and 25% in land (CS, vol. 1, fo. 1).

Cornelis Backer* declared his property at his marriage in 1655: 56% land and 44% bonds (GA, Backer papers, no. 77).

IN THE EARLY EIGHTEENTH CENTURY

Fifteen members of the elite died childless between 1701 and 1725 and a breakdown of their wealth is therefore recorded in CS. All figures are expressed in percentages.

Name	Date	Stock	Bonds	Houses	Land
A. Backer*	1701	–	41	55	4
D. Munter*	1701	50	12	20	18
C. Collen*	1704	60	40	–	–
J. Hudde*	1704	20	69	7	4
J. de Vries*	1708	23	62	9	6
F. W. van Loon*	1708	–	70	–	30
D. Bas*	1709	–	76	23	1
J. Bicker*	1713	1	95	–	4
D. Bernard*	1714	26	59	9	6
N. Witsen*	1717	10	80	5	5
J. Blocquery*	1719	71	14	15	–
A. Velters*	1719	68	25	7	0.3
N. Bambeeck*	1722	64	33	–	3
M. van Loon*	1723	9	58	22	11
J. de Haze*	1725	77	15	6	2

Bibliography

Addison, Joseph (1705) *Remarks on Several Parts of Italy*, London

Agostinetti, Giacomo (1679) *110 ricordi che formano il buon fattor di villa*; new edn Venice 1704

Agulhon, Maurice (1968) *Pénitents et franc-maçons dans l'ancienne Provence*, Paris

Aitzema, Lieuwe van (1657–68) *Saken van Staat en Oorlogh*; 2nd edn, 6 vols, The Hague 1669–72

Amelang, James S. (1986) *Honored Citizens of Barcelona: Patrician Culture and Class Relations, 1490–1714*, Princeton

Amelot de la Houssaie, Abraham Nicolas (1676) *Histoire du gouvernement de Venise*, Paris

Ariès, Philippe (1960) *Centuries of Childhood*, Eng. trans. London 1962

Arnaldi, Giorgio, and Manlio Pastore Stocchi, eds (1983) *Storia della cultura veneta dalla Controriforma alla fine della Repubblica*, Vicenza

Aymard, Maurice (1966) *Venise, Raguse et le commerce du blé*, Paris

Aymard, Maurice, ed. (1982) *Dutch Capitalism and World Capitalism*, Cambridge

Bacco, G., ed. (1856) *Relazione sulla organizzazione politica della Repubblica di Venezia*, Vicenza

Bachrach, P., and M. S. Baratz (1962) 'The Two Faces of Power',

American Political Science Review 56, 947–52

Backer, Joannes (1678) *Augustissimae societatis indiae orientalis encomium*, Amsterdam

Baiocchi, Angelo (1975–6) 'Paolo Paruta: ideologia e politica nel '500 veneziano', *SV* 17–18, 157–233

Bangs, Carl (1961) 'Arminius and the Reformation', *Church History* 30, 155–70

Bangs, Carl (1970) 'Dutch Theology, Trade and War 1590–1610', *Church History* 39, 470–82

Barbaro, Francesco (1513) *De re uxoria*, Paris; Eng. trans. 'On Wifely Duties', in *The Earthly Republic*, ed. Benjamin G. Kohl and Ronald G. Witt, London 1978, 189–228

'Il Barbaro', MS genealogies of the Venetian patriciate, copies in ASV, BCV

Barber, Elinor (1955) *The Bourgeoisie in Eighteenth-century France*, Princeton

Barbieri, Franco (1969) 'Le ville dello Scamozzi', *Bollettino Centro Andrea Palladio* 11, 222–9

Barbour, Violet (1950) *Capitalism in Amsterdam in the Seventeenth Century*, Baltimore

Bardi, Girolamo (1587) *Dichiaratione di tutte le istorie*, Venice

Barlaeus, Caspar (1632) *Mercator sapiens*, Amsterdam

Barpo, Gianbattista (1634) *Le delitie e i frutti dell'agricoltura e della villa*, Venice

Bassi, Elena (1968) *Architettura del '600 e del '700 a Venezia*, Naples

Battagia, Michele (1826) *Delle accademie veneziane*, Venice

Bellori, Pietro (1672) *Le vite de'pittori scultori e architetti moderni*, ed. Evelina Borea, Turin 1976

Belotti, Bortolo (1940) *Storia di Bergamo e dei bergamaschi*; 2nd edn Bergamo 1959

Beltrami, Daniele (1954) *Storia della popolazione di Venezia*, Padua

Beltrami, Daniele (1961) *Forze di lavoro e proprietà fondiaria nelle campagne venete*, Rome and Venice

Benzoni, Gino, and T. Zanato, eds (1982) *Storici e politici veneti del '500 e del '600*, Milan and Naples

Berengo, Marin (1956) *La società veneta alla fine del '700*, Florence

Beuningen, Coenraed van (1689) *Alle de brieven en schriften*, Amsterdam

Bistort, G. (1912) *Il magistrato alle pompe nella repubblica di Venezia*, Venice

Bitossi, Carlo (1976) 'Andrea Spinola', *Miscellanea Storia Liguria* 7, 115–75

Bitossi, Carlo (1990) *Il governo dei magnifici: patriziato e politica a Genova fra cinque e seicento*, Genoa

Blaeu, Joan (1662) *Geographia*, Amsterdam

Blankert, Albert (1982) *Ferdinand Bol*, Eng. trans. Doornspijk

Blok, Pieter J. ed. (1909) *Relazioni veneziane*, The Hague

Boccalini, Traiano (1910–48) *Ragguagli di Parnaso*, ed. G. Rua and L. Firpo, 3 vols, Bari

Bodin, Jean (1576) *Six Books of the Commonwealth*, Eng. trans. 1606, repr. Cambridge, MA, 1962

Bontemantel, Hans (1897) *De Regeering van Amsterdam*, ed. G. W. Kernkamp, 2 vols, The Hague

Borgherini-Scarabellin, N. (1917) *La vita privata a Padova nel secolo xvii*, Venice

Borlani, Antonia (1988) Introduzione to P. Burke, *Venezia e Amsterdam*, Bologna, 7–12

Boschini, Marco (1660) *Carta del navegar pittoresco*, Venice

Boschini, Marco (1664) *Le ricche minere della pittura*, Venice

Botero, Giovanni (1595) *Relatione della repubblica veneziana*, Venice

Bouman, J. (1856–7) *Bedijking, opkomst en bloei van de Boemster*, Purmerend

Bourdieu, Pierre (1972) *Outlines of a Theory of Practice*, Eng. trans. Cambridge 1977

Bourdieu, Pierre (1979) *Distinction*, Eng. trans. London 1981

Bouwsma, William J. (1968) *Venice and the Defense of Republican Liberty*, Berkeley and Los Angeles

Bracciolini, Poggio (1880) *Facetiae*, Paris

Brandt, Geeraerd (1682) *Leven van Vondel*; new edn Amsterdam 1932

Braudel, Fernand (1955) 'Note sull'economia del Mediterraneo nel 17 secolo', *Economia e storia* 2, 117–42

Braudel, Fernand (1958) 'History and the Social Sciences: the *Longue Durée*', in *On History*, Eng. trans. Chicago 1980, 25–54

Braudel, Fernand (1979) *The Perspective of the World*, Eng. trans. London 1983

Bredius, Abraham, et al. (1897–1905) *Amsterdam in de 17de eeuw*, 3 vols, The Hague

Bremmer, Jan, and Herman Roodenburg, eds (1991) *A Cultural History of Gesture*, Cambridge

Browning, Robert (1975) *Byzantium and Bulgaria*, London

Brugmans, Hajo (1897–1905) 'Handel en Nijverheid', in Bredius et al. (1897–1905), vol. 2

Burke, Peter, ed. (1967) *Sarpi*, New York

Burke, Peter (1978) *Popular Culture in Early Modern Europe*, London

Burke, Peter (1979) *Dutch Popular Culture in the Seventeenth Century*, Rotterdam

Burke, Peter (1982) 'Conspicuous Consumption in Seventeenth-century Italy', repr. as ch. 10 of *Historical Anthropology of Early Modern Italy*, Cambridge 1987

Burke, Peter (1987) Introduction to *The Social History of Language*, ed. Peter Burke and Roy Porter, Cambridge, 132–49

Burke, Peter (1991a) 'The Language of Gesture in Early Modern Italy', in Bremmer and Roodenburg (1991), 73–84

Burke, Peter (1991b) 'Reflections on Art Patronage in Venice and Amsterdam in the 16th and 17th Centuries', *Kunstlicht* 12: 2/3, 5–7

Burke, Peter (1992) *History and Social Theory*, Cambridge

Burke, Peter (1993a) 'Notes for a Social History of Silence in Early Modern Europe', in *The Art of Conversation*, Cambridge, 123–41

Burke, Peter (1993b) 'Prosopografie van de Renaissance', *Millennium* 7, 14–22

Burnet, Gilbert (1686) *Some Letters*, Rotterdam

Cameroni, Agostino (1893) *Uno scrittore avventuriero del secolo xvii*, n.p.

Campos, Elsa (1937) *I consorzi di bonifica nella repubblica veneta*, Padua

Canal, Bernardo (1908) 'Il collegio, l'ufficio e l'archivio dei dieci savi', *Nuovo Archivio Veneto*, n.s., 16, 115–50, 279–310

Capellari, G. A., 'Il Campidoglio Veneto', early-18th-century MS, BMV, It.VII.8304

Carasso-Kok, M., and J. Levy van Halm, eds (1988) *Schutters in*

Holland, Haarlem

Carleton, Dudley (1775) *Letters*, London

Carleton, Dudley (1992) 'The English Ambassador's Notes, 1612', in Chambers and Pullan (1992), 26–31

Carr, William (1688) *Remarks of the Government of Several Parts of Germany*, Amsterdam

Castiglione, Baldassare (1528) *The Courtier*, Eng. trans. New York 1959; I used the Turin 1964 edn, ed. Bruno Maier

Cats, Jacob (1624) *Houwelick*; I used the Amsterdam 1708 edn

Cervelli, Innocenzo (1966) 'Intorno alla decadenza di Venezia', *Nuova Rivista Storica* 50, 596–634

Chambers, David S. (1970) *The Imperial Age of Venice*, London

Chambers, David S., and Brian S. Pullan, eds (1992), *Venice: a Documentary History, 1450–1630*, Oxford

Cipolla, Carlo (1975) 'The Italian "Failure"', in *Failed Transitions to Modern Industrial Society*, ed. Frederick Krantz and Paul Hohenberg, Montreal, 8–10

Cipollato, Maria Teresa (1961) 'L'eredità di Federico Contarini', *SV* 3, 221–53

Colluraffi, Antonino (1623–33) *L'idea del gentilhuomo di repubblica overo il nobile veneto*, 2 vols, Venice

Commelin, Joan (1683) *Catalogus plantarum indigenarum hollandiae*, Amsterdam

Contarini, Gasparo (1543) *The Commonwealth and Government of Venice*, Eng. trans. 1599, repr. Amsterdam 1969; I used the Venice 1544 edn

Contarini, Nicolò (1576) *De perfectione rerum*; repr. Lyons 1587

Contarini, Nicolò (1982) 'Istorie veneziane', in Benzoni and Zanato (1982), 133–442

Coronelli, Vincenzo (1709) *La Brenta, luogo di delizie dei veneti patrizi*, Venice

Coryat, Thomas (1611) *Crudities*; repr., 2 vols, Glasgow 1905

Costantini, Claudio (1978) *La repubblica di Genova nell'età moderna*, Turin

Cowan, Alex F. (1982) 'Rich and Poor among the Patriciate in Early Modern Venice', *SV*, n.s., 6, 147–60

Cowan, Alex F. (1985) 'New Families in the Venetian Patriciate, 1646–1718', *Ateneo Veneto* 23

Cowan, Alex F. (1986) *The Urban Patriciate: Lübeck and Venice*

1580–1700, Cologne

Cozzi, Gaetano (1958) *Il doge Nicolò Contarini*, Venice and Rome

Cozzi, Gaetano (1959a) 'Appunti sul teatro e i teatri a Venezia agli inizi del '600', *SV* 1, 187–92

Cozzi, Gaetano (1959b) 'Paolo Sarpi tra il cattolico Phillippe Canaye de Fresnes e il calvinista Isaac Casaubon'; repr. in Cozzi (1979), 3-133

Cozzi, Gaetano (1961) 'Federico Contarini: un antiquario veneziano tra Rinascimento e Controriforma', *SV* 3, 190–220

Cozzi, Gaetano (1963–4) 'Cultura politica e religione nella pubblica storiografia veneziana', *SV* 5–6, 215–94

Cozzi, Gaetano (1979) *Paolo Sarpi tra Venezia e Europa*, Turin

Cozzi, Gaetano (1986) 'Venezia, una repubblica de'principi?' *SV*, n.s., 2, 139–57

Cracco, Giorgio (1967) *Società e stato nel medioevo veneziano*, Florence

Croll, Morris W. (1921) 'Attic Prose in the Seventeenth Century'; repr. in *Style, Rhetoric and Rhythm*, Princeton 1966, 51–101

Cutolo, Alessandro (1953) 'Un diario inedito del doge Leonardo Donà', *Nuova Antologia* 270–81

Cuyper, Abraham (1898) *Calvinism*; new edn London 1932

Dahl, Robert A. (1958) 'A Critique of the Ruling Elite Model', *American Political Science Review* 52, 463–9

Dahl, Robert A. (1961) *Who Governs?* New Haven

Davids, Karel, Jan Lukassen, and Jan Luiten van Zanden (1988) *De Nederlandse Geschiedenis als Afwijking van het Algemeen Menselijk Patroon*, Amsterdam

Davis, James C. (1962) *The Decline of the Venetian Nobility as a Ruling Class*, Baltimore

Davis, James C. (1975) *A Venetian Family and its Fortune*, Philadelphia

Dazzi, Manlio, ed. (1956) *Il fiore della lirica veneziana*, 3 vols, Venice

Dekker, Rudolf (1982) *Holland in Beroering: Oproeren in de 17de en 18de eeuw*, Baarn

Dekker, Rudolf, and Herman Roodenburg (1984) 'Humor in de zeventiende eeuw', *Tijdschrift voor Sociale Geschiedenis* 35, 243–66

Deursen, A. T. van (1974) *Bavianen en Slijkgeuzen*, Assen

Deursen, A. T. van (1978–80) *Plain Lives in a Golden Age*, Eng. trans. Cambridge 1991

Dibon, Paul (1954) *La philosophie néerlandaise au siècle d'or*, Paris

Dijk, Henk van, and Daniel J. Roorda (1971) 'Sociale mobiliteit onder regenten van de Republiek', *Tijdschrift voor Geschiedenis* 84, 306–28

Dillen, J. G. van, ed. (1929) *Bronnen tot de geschiedenis van het bedrijfsleven en het gildwesen van Amsterdam*, vol. 1, The Hague

Dillen, J. G. van, ed. (1941) *Amsterdam in 1585: het kohier der capitale impositie van 1585*, Amsterdam

Dillen, J. G. van, ed. (1958) *Het oudste aandeelhoudersregister van de kamer Amsterdam der Oost-Indische Compagnie*, The Hague

Dillen, J. G. van (1961) 'De West-Indische Compagnie, het Calvinisme en de Politiek', *Tijdschrift voor Geschiedenis* 74, 145–71

Dillen, J. G. van (1964) 'Amsterdam's Role in Seventeenth-century Dutch Politics and its Economic Background', in *Britain and the Netherlands*, vol. 2, ed. John S. Bromley and Ernst H. Kossman, Groningen, 133–47

Dillen, J. G. van (1970) *Van Rijkdom en Regenten*, The Hague

'Distinzioni segrete che corrono tra le casate nobili di Venezia', anonymous 17th-century MS, BMV, It.VII.2220

Dolfin, N. H. B. G. (1924) *I Dolfin*, Milan

Dore, Ronald P. (1965) *Education in Tokugawa Japan*, London

Douglas, Mary (1988) *Constructive Drinking*, London

Dudok van Heel, S. A. C. (1969) 'Het maecenaat de Graeff en Rembrandt', *Amstelodanum Maandblad*

Dudok van Heel, S. A. C. (1991a) 'Adellijke aristocratie in Venetië en burgerlike patriciaat in Amsterdam: het geslacht Donà en de familie Backer', in M. de Roever (1991), 66–85

Dudok van Heel, S. A. C. (1991b) *Van Maagschap tot factie*, Amsterdam

Durand, Yves (1973) *Les républiques au temps des monarchies*, Paris

Ehbrecht, Wilfried, ed. (1980) *Städtische Führungsgruppen und Gemeinde in der werdende Neuzeit*, Cologne and Vienna

Elias, Johan E. (1903–5) *De Vroedschap van Amsterdam, 1578–1795*, 2 vols, Haarlem

Elias, Johan E. (1923) *Geschiedenis van het Amsterdamsche Regentenpatriciaat*, The Hague

Elias, Johan E. (1937) *Het Geslacht Elias: een Amsterdamsche Regentenfamilie*, The Hague

Elias, Norbert (1939) *The Civilizing Process*, Eng. trans., 2 vols, Oxford 1978–82

Elias, Norbert (1969) *The Court Society*, Eng. trans. Oxford 1983

Elliott, John H. (1984) *Richelieu and Olivares*, Cambridge

Erikson, Erik H. (1950) *Childhood and Society*; rev. edn Harmondsworth 1965

Evenhuis, R. B. (1965–7) *Ook dat was Amsterdam*, 2 vols, Amsterdam

Faber, J. A. (1966) 'The Decline of the Baltic Grain-trade in the Second Half of the Seventeenth Century', *Acta Historiae Neerlandicae* 1, 108–31

Favaro, Antonio (1883) *Galileo Galilei e lo studio di Padova*, 2 vols, Florence

Favaro, Antonio (1891) 'Galileo Galilei e la presentazione del cannocchiale alla repubblica Veneta', *Nuovo Archivio Veneto* 1, 55–75

Favaro, Antonio (1893) 'Un ridotto scientifico in Venezia al tempo di Galileo Galilei', *Nuovo Archivio Veneto* 5, 199–209

Favaro, Antonio (1902) 'G. F. Sagredo e la vita scientifica in Venezia', *Nuovo Archivio Veneto*, n.s., 4, 313–87

Ferrarius, Omnibonus (1577) *De arte medica infantium*, Brescia

Fockema Andreae, S. J. (1961) *De Nederlandse Staat onder de Republiek*, Amsterdam

Fockema Andreae, S. J. and T. J. Meijer, eds (1968) *Album studiosorum academiae Franekerensis*, Franeker

Frank-van Westrienen, Anna (1983) *De Groote Tour: Tekening van de educatiereis der Nederlanders in de seventiende eeuw*, Amsterdam

Frederiks, J. G., and P. J. Frederiks, eds (1890) *Het kohier van 1631*, Amsterdam

Fremantle, Katherine (1959) *The Baroque Town Hall of Amsterdam*, Utrecht

Freschot, Camille (1709) *Nouvelle relation de la ville et république de Venise*, 3 vols, Utrecht

Fruin, Robert (1889) 'Bijdrage tot de geschiedenis van het burgermeesterschap van Amsterdam tijdens de republiek', *Bijdragen voor Vaderlandsche Geschiedenis*, 3rd ser., 5, 211–50

Gaeta, Franco (1964) 'Marcantonio Barbaro', in *Dizionario Biografico degli Italiani*, vol. 6, Rome, 110–2

García, Carlos (1617) *La oposición y conjunción de los dos grandes luminares de la tierra, o la antipatia de franceses y españoles*, ed. M. Bareau, Edmonton 1979

Gebhard, J. F. (1881) *Het Leven van mr Nicolaas Witsen*, Utrecht

Gelder, H. A. Enno van (1918) *De Levensbeschouwing van C. P. Hooft*, Amsterdam

Gelder, Roelof van (1993) 'Les messieurs XVII', in Méchoulan (1993), 82–102

Georgelin, Jean (1968) 'Une grande propriété en Vénétie au 18e siècle: Anguillara', *Annales: economies, sociétés, civilisations* 27, 483–517

Georgelin, Jean (1973) 'Ordres et classes à Venise au 17e et 18e siècles', in *Ordres et classes*, ed. Camille-Ernest Labrousse, Paris, 193–7

Georgelin, Jean (1978) *Venise au siècle des lumières*, The Hague

Ginzburg, Carlo (1976) *Cheese and Worms*, Eng. trans. London 1980

Ginzburg, Carlo (1989) *Ecstasies*, Eng. trans. London 1990

Gluckman, Max (1956) *Custom and Conflict in Africa*, Oxford

Goffman, Erving (1959) *The Presentation of Self in Everyday Life*, New York

Grendi, Edoardo (1976) *Introduzione alla storia moderna della repubblica di Genova*, Genoa

Groenhuis, G. (1981) 'Calvinism and National Consciousness: the Dutch Republic as the New Israel', in *Britain and the Netherlands*, vol. 7, ed. Alastair Duke and C. A. Tamse, The Hague, 118–33

Gualdo Priorato, Galeazzo (1659) *Scena d'alcuni uomini illustri*, Venice

Haitsma Mulier, Eco O. G. (1980) *The Myth of Venice and Dutch*

Republican Thought in the Seventeenth Century, Assen

Haks, Donald (1983) *Huwelijk en gezin in Holland in de 17de en 18de eeuw*; 2nd edn Utrecht 1985

Hale, John R. (1973) 'Military Academies on the Venetian *Terraferma* in the Early Seventeenth Century', *SV* 15, 273–95

Haskell, Francis (1963) *Patrons and Painters*; rev. edn New Haven and London 1980

Havard, Henri (1876) *Amsterdam et Venise*, Paris

Haverkamp-Begemann, Egbert (1982) *Rembrandt: 'The Nightwatch'*, Princeton

Heckscher, William S. (1958) *Rembrandt's 'Anatomy of Dr Nicolas Tulp', an Iconographical Study*, New York

Heemskerck, Johan van (1637) *Batavische Arcadia*, Amsterdam

Hoboken, W. J. van (1960) 'The Dutch West India Company: the Political Background of its Rise and Decline', in *Britain and the Netherlands*, vol. 1, ed. John S. Bromley and Ernst H. Kossman, London, 41–61

Hobsbawm, Eric J. (1954) 'The Crisis of the Seventeenth Century'; repr. in *Crisis in Europe 1560–1660*, ed. Trevor Aston, London 1965, 5–58

Hooft, Cornelis P. (1871–1925) *Memoriën en Adviesen*, 2 vols, Utrecht

Hooft, Pieter C. (1626) *Baeto*, Amsterdam

Hooft, Pieter C. (1649) *Rampseligheden der Verheffinge van den huize van Medicis*; new edn Amsterdam 1661

Houbraken, Arnold (1718–21) *De Groote Schouwburg van Schildern en Schilderinnen*; new edn, 3 vols, Maastricht 1944

Houtzager, D. (1950) *Hollands Lijf- en Losrenteleningen vóór 1672*, Schiedam

Howard, Deborah (1975) *Jacopo Sansovino: Architecture and Patronage in Renaissance Venice*, New Haven and London

Howe, Daniel W. (1972) 'The Decline of Calvinism', *Comparative Studies in Society and History* 14, 306–27

Howell, James (1651) *Epistolae Ho-ellianae*, London

Hudde, Joannes (1659) 'De reductione aeguationum' and 'De maximis et minimis', in René Descartes, *Geometria*, ed. F. Schooten, Leiden

Huizinga, Johan (1932) *Dutch Civilization in the 17th Century*, Eng. trans. London 1968

Huizinga, Johan (1938) *Homo Ludens*, Eng. trans. 1949, repr. London 1970

Impey, Oliver, and Arthur Macgregor, eds (1985) *The Origins of Museums: the Cabinet of Curiosities in 16th- and 17th-century Europe*, Oxford

Israel, Jonathan I. (1985) *European Jewry in the Age of Mercantilism*, Oxford

Israel, Jonathan I. (1989) *Dutch Primacy in World Trade*, Oxford

Ivanovitch, Cristoforo (1681) *Minerva al tavolino*, Venice

Jonge, J. C. de (1852) *Nederland en Venetië*, The Hague

Jongh, Eddie de (1985), review of B. Haak, *The Golden Age*, *Simiolus* 15, 65–8

Kalff, Gerrit (1895) *Literatur en tooneel te Amsterdam in de 17de eeuw*, Haarlem

Kalff, Gerrit (1906–12) *Geschiedenis der Nederlandsche Letterkunde*, 9 vols, Groningen

Kellenbenz, Hermann (1958) 'Der italienische Grosskaufmann und die Renaissance', *Vierteljahrschrift für Sozial- und Wirtschaftsgeschichte* 45, 145–67

Kernkamp, G. W. (1897) 'Historie en Regeering', in Bredius et al. (1897–1905)

Kernkamp, Johannes Hermann (1931–4) *De handel op den vijand 1572–1609*, 2 vols, Utrecht

Kistemaker, R., and M. Jonker (1986) *De smaak van de elite*, Amsterdam

Klein, Melanie (1960) *Our Adult World and its Roots in Infancy*, London

Klein, Pieter W. (1965) *De Trippen in de 17de eeuw*, Assen

Knuttel, W. P. C., ed. (1889–1920) *Catalogus van de Pamletten Verzameling berustende in de Koninklijke Bibliotheek*, 9 vols, The Hague

Koeman, C. (1970) *Joan Blaeuw and his Grand Atlas*, Amsterdam

Kolakowski, Leszek (1965) *Chrétiens sans église*, Fr. trans. Paris 1969

Le Roy Ladurie, Emmanuel (1966) *The Peasants of Languedoc*, abbreviated Eng. trans. Urbana 1975

Le Roy Ladurie, Emmanuel (1975) *Montaillou*, Eng. trans. London 1976

Leth, Andries de (1719) *De zegepralende Vecht*, Amsterdam

Levi, Cesare Augusto (1900) *Le collezioni veneziane d'arte e d'antichità*, Venice

Levi, Giovanni (1991) 'On Microhistory', in *New Perspectives on Historical Writing*, ed. P. Burke, Cambridge, 93–113

Levine, Joseph M. (1977) *Dr Woodward's Shield*, Berkeley

Lewis, Archibald R. (1974) *Knights and Samurai*, London

Litta, Pompeo (1819) *Celebri famiglie italiane*, Milan

Logan, Anne-Marie (1991) 'Kunstenaars, kooplieden en verzamelaars', in M. de Roever (1991), 137–55

Logan, Oliver (1972) *Culture and Society in Venice, 1470–1790*, London

Loredan, Gianfrancesco (1635) *Discorsi academici*, Venice

Loredan, Gianfrancesco (1676) *Bizarrie academiche*, Bologna

Lowry, Martin J. C. (1971) 'The Church and Political Change in the Later '500', Ph.D. thesis, University of Warwick

Lowry, Martin J. C. (1972) 'The Reform of the Council of Ten', *SV* 14

Lupis, Antonio (1663) *Vita di Gianfrancesco Loredano*, Venice

Luttervelt, Remmet B. R. van (1943) *De buitenplaatsen aan de Vecht*, Utrecht

Luzzatto, Gino (1958) *An Economic History of Italy*, Eng. trans. London 1961

Mabilleau, Léopold (1881) *Cesare Cremonini*, Paris

Macfarlane, Alan (1978) *The Origins of English Individualism*, Oxford

Mallett, Michael E., and John R. Hale (1984) *The Military Organization of a Renaissance State: Venice, c.1400 to 1617*, Cambridge

Manfredi, Fulgenzio (1602) *Degnità procuratoria di Venezia*, Venice

Maranini, Giuseppe (1931) *La costituzione di Venezia dopo la serrata del Maggior Consiglio*, Venice

Mastellone, Salvatore (1983) 'Holland as a Political Model in Italy in the Seventeenth Century', *Bijdragen en Mededelingen betreffende de geschiedenis der Nederlanden* 98, 568–82

Mattozzi, Ivo (1977) review of Peter Burke, *Venice and Amsterdam*, *SV*, n.s., 1, 217–24

Mazzotti, Giuseppe, ed. (1953) *Le ville venete*, Treviso

Mazzotti, Giuseppe (1957) *Venetian Villas*, Rome

Méchoulan, Henry, ed. (1993) *Amsterdam 17e siècle*, Paris

Meier Drees, Marijke (1989) *De treurspelen van Thomas Asselijn*, Enschede

Mills, C. Wright (1956) *The Power Elite*, New York

Misson, François Maximilien (1691–8) *Nouveau voyage d'Italie*, 3 vols, The Hague

Molin, Francesco da, 'Compendio', 17th-century MS, BMV, It.VII.8812

Molmenti, Pompeo (1879) *History of Venice in Private Life*, Eng. trans. 6 vols, London 1906–8

Molmenti, Pompeo (1919) *Curiosità di storia veneziana*, Bologna

Moltke, Joachim Wolfgang von (1965) *Govaert Flink*, Amsterdam

Morgan, Edmund S. (1944) *The Puritan Family*; new edn New York 1966

Moryson, Fynes (1907–8) *An Itinerary*, 4 vols, Glasgow

Moschini, Giovanni Antonio (1842) *La chiesa e il seminario di S. Maria della Salute*, Venice

Mosto, Alvise da (1960) *I dogi di Venezia*, Milan

Mousnier, Roland (1969) *Social Hierarchies*, Eng. trans. New York 1973

Muinck, B. E. (1967) 'A Regent's Family Budget about the Year 1700', *Acta Historiae Neerlandicae* 2, 222–32

Muller, Samuel (1941) *Schetsen uit de middeleeuwen*, 2 vols, Amsterdam

Murris, R. (1925) *La Hollande et les hollandais au 17e et au 18e siècle vus par les français*, Paris

Nani, Battista (1662) *Historia della repubblica veneta*, Venice

Nani Mocenigo, F. (1894) *Agostino Nani*, Venice

Nani Mocenigo, Mario (1935) *Storia della marina veneziana da Lepanto alla caduta della repubblica*, Rome

Nicholson, Ralph W. (1969) 'Factions: a Comparative Analysis', in *Political Systems and the Distribution of Power*, ed., Michael Banton, London, 21–61

Nielsen, Axel (1933) *Dänische Wirtschaftsgeschichte*, Jena

Nierop, Henk F. K. van (1984) *The Nobility of Holland: from Knights to Regents, 1500–1650*, Eng. trans. Cambridge 1993

Notestein, Robert B. (1968) 'The Patrician', *International Journal of Comparative Sociology* 9, 106–20

Oldewelt, Willem F. H., ed. (1945) *Het kohier van 1742*,

Amsterdam

Ossowski, Stanislaw (1957) *Class Structure in the Social Consciousness*, Eng. trans. London 1963

Overbeke, Aernout van (1991) *Anecdota sive historiae jocosae*, ed. Rudolf Dekker and Herman Roodenburg, Amsterdam

Pareto, Vilfredo (1916) *The Mind and Society*, Eng. trans. London 1935

Parival, Jean Nicolas de (1661) *Les délices de la Hollande*; rev. edn Amsterdam 1669

Parker, Geoffrey, and Lesley M. Smith, eds (1978) *The General Crisis of the Seventeenth Century*, London

Parry, Geraint (1969) *Political Elites*, London

Parry, Jonathan (1984) *Aristocracy*, London

Paruta, Paolo (1579) *Perfettione della vita politica*, Venice

Patriziati e aristocrazie (1978), Trento

Piccioli, Francesco Maria (1685) *L'Orologio del piacere*, Piazzola

Piccioli, Francesco Maria (1679) *Le Amazzone nell'isole fortunate*, Padua

Piovene, Guido, and L. Magagnato, eds (1960) *Ville del Brenta nelle vedute di Vincenzo Coronelli e Gianfrancesco Costa*, Milan

Pomian, Krzysztof (1987) *Collectors and Curiosities: Paris and Venice, 1500–1800*, Eng. trans. Cambridge 1990

Porta, Antonio (1975) *Joan en Gerrit Corver: de Politieke Macht van Amsterdam*, Assen

Porter, Roy (1991) 'The History of the Body', in *New Perspectives in Historical Writing*, ed. Peter Burke, Cambridge

Posthumus, Nicolaas W. (1943–64) *Nederlandsche Prijsgeschiedenis*, 2 vols, Leiden

Prak, Maarten, J. de Jong, and L. Kooijmans (1985) 'State and Status in the Eighteenth Century', in Schilling and Diederiks (1985),183–93

Price, J. Lesley (1974) *Culture and Society in the Dutch Republic during the Seventeenth Century*, London

Pullan, Brian S. (1963–4) review of James C. Davis (1962), *SV* 5–6, 406–25

Pullan, Brian S. (1964) 'Service to the Venetian State: Aspects of Myth and Reality in the Early Seventeenth Century', *Studi Secenteschi* 5, 95–147

Pullan, Brian S., ed. (1968) *Crisis and Change in the Venetian Economy in the 16th and 17th Centuries*, London

Pullan, Brian S. (1971) *Rich and Poor in Renaissance Venice*, Oxford

Pullan, Brian S. (1973) 'The Occupations and Investments of the Venetian Nobility in the Middle and Late Sixteenth Century', in *Renaissance Venice*, ed. John R. Hale, London, 379–408

Puppi, Lionello (1973) *Andrea Palladio*, Eng. trans. London 1975

Quondam, Amedeo (1982) 'L'accademia', in *Letteratura Italiana*, ed. Alberto Asor Rosa, vol. 1, Turin, 823–98

Raeff, Marc (1966) *Origins of the Russian Intelligentsia: the Eighteenth-century Nobility*, New York

Rapp, Richard T. (1975) 'The Unmaking of the Mediterranean Trade Hegemony', *Journal of Economic History* 35, 499–525

Rapp, Richard T. (1976) *Industry and Economic Decline in Seventeenth-century Venice*, Cambridge, MA

Rapp, Richard T. (1979) 'Real Estate and Rational Investment in Early Modern Venice', *Journal of European Economic History* 8, 269–90

Ravesteyn, Willem van (1906) *Onderzoekingen over de economische en sociale ontwikkeling van Amsterdam*, Amsterdam

Reael, Laurens (1651) *Observatien aen de magnetsteen*, Amsterdam

Redlich, Fritz (1958) 'Toward Comparative Historiography', *Kyklos* 11, 362–88

Relatione 1. 'Relatione della città e repubblica di Venezia', anonymous 17th-century MS, BL, Add.10,130

Relatione 2. 'Relatione del politico governo di Venezia', anonymous 17th-century MS, BL, Add.18,660

Relatione 3. 'Relatione di tutti le renditi e spese che la repubblica di Venezia ordinariamente cava', anonymous 17th-century MS, BL, Add.18,660

Renier, Gustaaf J. (1944) *The Dutch Nation*, London

Rhede van der Kloot, M. A. van (1891) *De gouverneurs-generaal van Nederlands-Indië*, The Hague

Ridolfi, Carlo (1648) *Le maraviglie dell'arte*, 2 vols, Venice

Rietbergen, Peter J. A. N. (1986) 'Witsen's World', in *All of One Company: the VOC in Biographical Perspective*, ed. R. Ross and G. D. Winius, Utrecht

Rieu, W. N. du, ed. (1875) *Album studiosorum academiae Lugduni Batavae*, The Hague

Roche, Daniel (1989) *La culture des apparences: une histoire du vêtement, 17e–18e siècles*, Paris

Rodenwalt, Ernst (1957) 'Untersuchungen über die Biologie des venezianisches Adels', *Homo* 8, 1–26

Roever, Margriet de, ed. (1991) *Amsterdam: Venetië van het Noorden*, Amsterdam

Roever, Nicolaas de, ed. (1882) *Album Academicum van het Athenaeum Illustre*, Amsterdam

Roever, Nicolaas de (1889) 'Tweeërlei Regenten', *Oud-Holland* 7, 63-88

Rohan, Duc de (1661) *Mémoires*, 2 vols, Paris

Roldanus, Cornelia Wilhelmina (1931) *Coenraad van Beuningen*, The Hague

Romanin, Samuele (1853–61) *Storia documentata di Venezia*, 10 vols, Venice

Romano, Ruggiero (1968) 'Italia nella crisis del secolo xvii', *Studi Storici* 9, 723–41

Romein, Jan (1934) *De lage landen bij de Zee*, Utrecht

Roodenburg, Herman (1990) *Onder Censuur: de kerkelijke tucht in de gereformeerde gemeente van Amsterdam, 1578–1700*, Hilversum

Roorda, Daniel J. (1961) *Partij en factie*, Groningen

Roorda, Daniel J. (1964) 'The Ruling Class in Holland in the Seventeenth Century', in *Britain and the Netherlands*, vol. 2, ed. John S. Bromley and Ernst H. Kossman, Groningen, 109–32

Rosa, Salvatore (1939) *Lettere inedite*, ed. A. de Rinaldis, Rome

Rose, Charles J. (1974) 'Marc Antonio Venier, Renier Zeno and the Myth of Venice', *The Historian* 36, 479–97

Rosenberg, Hans (1958) *Bureaucracy, Aristocracy and Autocracy: the Prussian Experience 1660–1815*, Cambridge, MA

Rowen, Herbert H. (1986) *John de Witt*, Cambridge

Sagredo, Giovanni (1655) (under the pseudonym Ginnesio Gavardo Vacalerio) *Arcadia in Brenta*; new edn Venice 1669

Sagredo, Giovanni (1673) *Memorie istoriche de' monarchi ottomani*, Venice

Saint-Didier, Alexandre Limojon de (1680) *La ville et la république de Venise*, 3nd edn, Amsterdam

Sansovino, Francesco (1663) *Venetia città nobilissima*, rev. by G. Martinioni, Venice

Sarpi, Paolo (1624) *Istoria dell'interdetto*; repr. Bari 1940

[Sarpi, Paolo, attributed] (1788) *Opinione toccante il governo della repubblica veneziana*, London

Savelli, Rodolfo (1981) *La repubblica oligarchica*, Milan

Savini-Branca, Simona (1964) *Il collezionismo veneziano nel '600*, Padua

Sayous, André E (1940) 'Le patriciat d'Amsterdam', *Annales d'histoire sociale*, 177–98

Scamozzi, Vincenzo (1615) *Idea dell'architettura universale*, Venice

Scazzoso, Mario (1985) 'Nobiltà senatoria e nobiltà minore a Venezia fra sei e settecento', *Nuova Rivista Storica* 69, 503–30

Schaep, Gerard (1655) 'Alloquium ad filios'; repr. in *Bijdragen en Mededelingen van de Historische Genootschap* 16 (1895), 333–71

Schama, Simon (1987) *The Embarrassment of Riches*, London

Schilling, Heinz, and Herman Diederiks, eds (1985) *Bürgerliche Eliten*, Cologne and Vienna

Schöffer, Ivo (1964) 'Did Holland's Golden Age Coincide with a Period of Crisis?', Eng. trans. in Parker and Smith (1978), 83–109

Schöffer, Ivo (1968) 'La stratification sociale de la république des Provinces-Unies au 17e siècle', in *Problèmes de Stratification Sociale*, ed. Roland Mousnier, 121-32

Schöffer, Ivo (1975) 'The Batavian Myth', in *Britain and the Netherlands*, vol. 5, ed. John S. Bromley and Ernst H. Kossman, The Hague, 78-101

Scholte, J. H. (1916) 'Philipp von Zesen', *Jaarboek Amstelodanum* 14

Schraa, P. (1954) 'Onderzoekingen naar de bevolkingsomvang van Amsterdam, 1550-1650', *Jaarboek Amstelodanum* 46, 1–27

Schumpeter, Joseph (1943) *Capitalism, Socialism and Democracy*, London

Schwartz, Gary (1985) *Rembrandt: his Life, his Paintings*, New York

Selden, John (1892) *Table-talk*, Oxford

Sella, Domenico (1957) 'The Rise and Fall of the Venetian Woollen Industry', rev. Eng. version in Pullan (1968), 106–26

Sella, Domenico (1959) 'Crisis and Transformation in Venetian Trade', rev. Eng. version in Pullan (1968), 88–105

Sella, Domenico (1961) Commerci e industrie a Venezia nel secolo xvii, Venice and Rome

Seneca, Federico (1959) Leonardo Donà, Padua

Sidney, Henry (1843) Diary of the Times of Charles II, ed. R. W. Blencowe, 2 vols, London

Simioni, A. (1968) Storia di Padova, Padua

Six, Jan (1648) Medea, Amsterdam

Skocpol, Theda (1979) States and Social Revolutions, Cambridge

Smith, Adam (1776) Wealth of Nations; I used the London 1904 edn

Snowman, Daniel (1977) Kissing Cousins, London

Spierenburg, Pieter (1981) Elites and Etiquette, Rotterdam

Spierenburg, Pieter (1984) The Spectacle of Suffering, Cambridge

Spini, Giorgio (1950) Ricerca dei libertini; 2nd edn Florence 1983

Stella, Aldo (1956) 'La crisi economica veneziana della seconda metà del secolo xvi', Archivio Veneto 58-9, 17–69

Stella, Aldo (1964) Chiesa e stato nelle relazioni dei nunzi pontifici a Venezia, Vatican City

Stella, Aldo (1967) Dall'anabattismo al socianesimo nel '500, Padua

Stone, Lawrence (1965) The Crisis of the English Aristocracy (1558–1641), Oxford

Stone, Lawrence (1971) 'Prosopography', repr. in The Past and the Present Revisited, London 1987, 45–73

Storia della cultura veneta (1981–5), vols 3–5, Padua

Tafuri, Manfredo (1985) Venice and the Renaissance, Eng. trans. Cambridge, MA, 1989

Tagliaferri, Amelio, ed. (1984) I ceti dirigenti in Italia, Udine

Taviani, Francesco, ed. (1970) La commedia dell'arte e la società barocca: la fascinazione del teatro, Rome

Temple, William (1673) Observations upon the United Provinces, ed. George N. Clark, Cambridge 1932

Tenenti, Alberto (1959) 'Il De perfectione rerum di Nicolò Contarini', SV 1, 155–66

Tenenti, Alberto (1961) Piracy and the Decline of Venice, Eng.

trans. London 1967

Terpstra, H. (1960) *Jacob van Neck*, Amsterdam

Thijssen-Schoutte, C. Louise (1954) *Nederlands Cartesianisme*, Amsterdam

Thomas, Keith V. (1977) 'The Place of Laughter in Tudor and Stuart England', *Times Literary Supplement* 21 January

Thompson, Edward P. (1963) *The Making of the English Working Class*, London

Tiepolo, Giovanni (1617) *Trattato delle santissime reliquie ultimamente ritrovate nel santuario della chiesa di San Marco*, Venice

Tomasi di Lampedusa, Giuseppe (1958) *Il gattopardo*; new edn Milan 1966

Trevelyan, George M. (1942) *English Social History*, London

Trevisan, Bernardo (1704) *Meditazioni filosofiche*, Venice

Trip, Joannes (1681) *Oratio metrica de civium concordiae necessitate*, Amsterdam

Tulp, Nicolaes (1641) *Observationes medicae*, Amsterdam

[Venier, Zuanantonio, attributed] 'Storia delle rivolutioni seguite nel governo della Repubblica di Venezia', 17th-century MS, BCV, Cicogna 3762

Ventura, Angelo (1964) *Nobiltà e popolo nella società veneta del '400 e '500*, Bari

Ventura, Angelo (1968) 'Consideration sull'agricoltura veneta nei secoli xvi e xvii', *Studi Storici* 9, 674–722

Ventura, Angelo (1969) 'Aspetti storico-economici della villa veneta', *Bollettino Centro Andrea Palladio* 11, 65–75

Vianello, Nereo (1957) 'Il veneziano, lingua del foro veneto', *Lingua Nostra* 18, 67–73

Vingboons, Philips (1688) *Gronden en afbeeldsels der voornaamste gebouwen*, Amsterdam

Völger, G., and Karen v. Welck, eds (1990) *Männerbande, Männerbünde*, Köln

Vondel, Joost van (1662) *Batavische Gebroeders*, Amsterdam

Vos, Jan (1726) *Alle de Gedichten*, Amsterdam

Vossius, Gerard (1632) 'De historiae utilitate'; repr. in *Opera Omnia*, vol. 4, Amsterdam 1699, 94–9

Waal, Henri van de (1952) *Drie eeuwen vaderlandsche Geschieduitbeelding*, The Hague

Waard, C. de (1911) 'Joannes Hudde', *NNBW*, vol. 1, Leiden

Wagenaar, Jan (1779) *Amsterdam*, Amsterdam

Wiel, Taddeo (1888) *I codici musicali contariniani*, Venice

Wilson, Charles (1970) *Queen Elizabeth and the Revolt of the Netherlands*, London

Witsen, Nicolaes (1671) *Scheepsbouw en bestier*, Amsterdam

Witsen, Nicolaes (1705) *Noord en Oost Tartarye*, 2nd edn, Amsterdam

Witsen, Nicolaes (1872) 'Kort verhaal van mijn levensloop', in *Aemstel's Oudheid*, ed. P. Scheltema, vol. 6, 40–51

Witsen, Nicolaes (1966–7) *Moscovische Reyse, 1664–5*, ed. T. J. G. Locher and P. de Buck, 3 vols, The Hague

Woolf, Stuart J. (1962) 'Venice and the *Terraferma*', in Pullan (1968), 175–203

Wootton, David (1983) *Paolo Sarpi*, Cambridge

Worp, Jacob Adolf (1879) *Jan Vos*, Groningen

Worp, Jacob Adolf (1904–8) *Geschiedenis van het drama in Nederland*, 2 vols, Groningen

Worsthorne, Simon T. (1954) *Venetian Opera in the 17th Century*, Oxford

Woude, A. M. van der (1972) 'Variations in the Size and Structure of the Household in the United Provinces of the Netherlands in the Seventeenth and Eighteenth Centuries', in *Household and Family in Past Time*, ed. Peter Laslett, Cambridge, 299–318

Yriarte, Charles (1885) *Un patricien de Venise*, Paris

Zeno, P. A. (1662) *Memoria de' scrittori veneti patritii*, Venice

Zesen, Philipp von (1645) *Adriatische Rosemund*, Amsterdam

Zesen, Philipp von (1664) *Beschreibung der Stadt Amsterdam*, Amsterdam

Zumthor, Paul (1959) *Daily Life in Rembrandt's Holland*, Eng. trans. London 1962

Index